25th
ANNIVERSARY
EDITION

BRADYMANIA!

Everything You Always Wanted to Know — and a Few Things You Probably Didn't

by Elizabeth Moran

D1435786

ADAMS PUBLISHING
Holbrook, Massachusetts

Published by Adams Media Corporation
260 Center Street, Holbrook, MA 02343

ISBN: 1-55850-418-4

Printed in the United States of America

C   D   E   F   G   H   I   J

This publication was not created by, nor has it been authorized by, Paramount Studios or
ABC-TV.

Library of Congress Cataloging-in-Publication Data
    Moran, Elizabeth.
    Bradymania! :   everything you always wanted to know—and a few things you
probably didn't / Elizabeth Moran. —   25th anniversary ed.
       p.   cm.
    Includes bibliographical references.
    ISBN 1-55850-418-4
    1. Brady bunch (television program)   I.   Title.
PN1992.77.B733M67   1994
791.45\72—dc20   94-35376
                                        CIP

*This book is available at quantity discounts for bulk purchases.
For information, call 1-800-872-5627.*

TABLE OF CONTENTS

Introduction 7

PART ONE: HERE'S THE STORY

The Characters 13
Brady Family Tree 32
"The Brady Bunch" Episode Summary 33
The Cast, Then and Now 76
The Real Head of the Brady Family: Sherwood
    Schwartz 121
4222 Clinton Way—The Happiest Place On
    Earth! 124
Did You Ever Wonder 129

PART TWO: THE WAY THEY ALL BECAME
THE BRADY BUNCH

In the Beginning 133
    The Birth of "The Brady Bunch" 133
    Casting the Bunch 136
    Brady Mechanics: The Production 140
    Educating The Bradys: School Life. 141
    Recreation, Brady Style. 144

The Brady Phenomenon 145

The Fall of the House of Brady................. 146

The Ultimate Brady Bunch Trivia Challenge 149

Trivia Challenge (Answers)................... 165

Who Said This 166

Who Said This (Answers) 175

Mistakes That Slipped Past 176

Brady Nepotism 178

The Grand Canyon Quiz 181

The Grand Canyon Quiz (Answers) 181

What's My Name, Part 1 182

What's My Name, Part 1 (Answers)............. 182

What's My Name, Part 2 183

What's My Name, Part 2 (Answers)............. 183

PART THREE: MUCH MORE THAN A HUNCH

Brady Bunch Collectibles......................... 187

The Brady Kids, Live In Concert.................... 199

Brady TV Spinoffs 204

The Brady Legend Lives On 218

"The Brady Bunch": The New Movie 223

The Brady Bunch Family Album.................... 229

Photo and Illustration Credits....................... 236

Bibliography..................................... 238

ACKNOWLEDGMENTS

A standing ovation to the individuals who shared their time, memories, and photos, and who truly made *Bradymania!* possible: Sherwood Schwartz, Florence Henderson, Barry Williams, Mike Lookinland, Susan Olsen, Ann B. Davis, Robbie Rist, Allan Melvin, Karen Lipscomb, Joe Seiter, Mrs. Whitfield, Johnnie J. Young, Stephen Cox, and my agent, Jim Pinkston, who really believed in this project and never gave up!

I am also extremely thankful to the following people: Diane Albert, Leah Ayres, Jeff Botcher, David E. Brady, Rose Blume, Barbara Chase, Terri Collins, David Colman, Frank Delfino, Howard Frank, Larry Germain, Robert Greenhood, Susan Grushkin, Kathy Hill, Melanie Hutsell, Frank Inn, Dana Jaeger, Hope Juber, Michael Lerner at the Toy Patrol, Sid Mailhes, Monty Margetts, Peter Mathes, Mrs. McCallister, Michael Mealiffe, Max Merlin, Scott J. Michaels, Karl Miller, Bill Morgan, Pat Mullins, Eve Plumb, Sherry Robb, Mark Robert, Darlene Schwartz, Erin and Don Smith, Jill and Faith Soloway, Scott Sullivan, Lisa Sutton, Becky Thyre, and Debra de Waltoff.

And thanks go as well to my friends Lamar, Sara and Fergus, Maura, Marty, Richard, D. Scott, Ron, Lynetta, Jeff and Sharon, the O'Connor School of Irish Dance, and my husband Valeriy, for being so supportive.

Finally, *Bradymania!* really wouldn't be possible if it weren't for my editor Brandon Toropov, and Christopher Ciaschini, Dawn Hobson, and Kate Layzer of Bob Adams, Inc.

❁   ❁   ❁

For Alicia and Brendan

❁   ❁   ❁

INTRODUCTION

What is it about "The Brady Bunch" that keeps people coming back for more?

The show's many fans are the last to claim that it is "great television," whatever that is. Those who weren't part of the program's generation (as of this writing, the cutoff age seems to be a year or two under 35) are often surprised to hear their younger friends praising, with a wry smile, the very same aspects of the program—the stereotyping, the lameness of the jokes, the tacky clothes, the virtually content-free upper-middle-class lifestyle—that would seem to be the biggest obstacles to its enjoyment.

All agree that "The Brady Bunch" was an occasionally (okay, more than occasionally) formulaic part of late-Sixties, early-Seventies America. It featured six cute kids who managed to cause a lot of harmless trouble, who lived in a world where everything turned out well in the end. Each of the cute kids had lost a parent and gotten another one, but the new arrangement seemed to work—seemed to work so well, in fact, that the old family configurations were virtually never mentioned. Problems had to do, not with dislocation or loss, as you might expect, but with things like becoming the next Shirley Temple or finding a lost dog. The show was, to quote lead actor Robert Reed (Mike Brady), " 'Gilligan's Island' with kids." It was straight-up, unapologetic, mainstream commercial television meant to be viewed before bedtime at nine.

Yet Brady partisans, who often seem to be *everyone* who was born after about 1960 and had access to a television, persist in finding the show charming and a heck of a lot of fun. More to the point, they still watch it. A lot. Whether the image is of a four-year-old glued to the reruns for the first time or a thirty-year-old watching as a trip down memory lane, there is still a huge audience for "The Brady Bunch" . . . no matter what the show's detractors had or have to say about it.

Why? The show was designed for children, of course; whatever else can be said about it, there can be no doubt now that it spoke—and speaks—to that audience with great effectiveness. There is a seemingly endless wave of young viewers who are fascinated by "The Brady Bunch" for the same reason many of their parents were at their age. It deals with issues like honesty, sibling rivalry, popularity, and a dawning interest in the opposite sex in a gentle, unpretentious way. It is utterly without hidden meanings. There is no attempt at social significance. "The Brady Bunch" is, for 1990s children as it was for 1970s children, a look at family life that is so artificial as to be completely unthreatening. (During its initial run, the show's producers had to come up with a form letter gently dissuading the hundreds of kids who wrote to express their wish to run away from home and join the Brady family.)

As for the adults, our fascination with the Bunch may have more to do with a certain wistful, contradictory look back at our own childhoods, a look that is, on the whole, probably not unhealthy—since it beats ignoring the past altogether. The Bradys are ridiculous, and we know that, yet in a way we still envy them terribly. The show we summon up again and again is dated, narrow-minded, insulated from reality, often unintentionally hilarious—but so are dozens of other sitcoms from the era. No one is resurrecting old scripts of "Nanny and the Professor" for off-Broadway theatrical runs (at least not yet). The difference is that "The Brady Bunch" represented the family we wanted to belong to—and didn't. What if we had?

The generation now in its late twenties and early thirties bore the brunt of a skyrocketing divorce rate, the sudden necessity of two incomes to maintain the family lifestyle one used to support, and the rise (or was it simply the acknowledgment?) of the dysfunctional family in what used to be called Middle America. *Why* are we still amused and, yes, entranced by a vaguely affluent, impossibly perfect family that accompanied them through adolescence? It's a little like Louis Armstrong's definition of jazz: If you have to ask, we can't tell you.

And hey, if the Bunch was insulated from the shocks of the real world, was that really so bad? Isn't that exactly what we were (and perhaps still are) after? Doesn't the memory of their so-called "mindless" problems—getting a date, finding the best way to keep a promise, wearing braces for the first time, being overshadowed by an older sibling—

call to mind a time in our lives when these really were the most important issues of the day? Is there anything wrong with enjoying that feeling again for half an hour every now and then—while we make fun of the miniskirts and perms?

You can only go so far with all this, of course. Wallpaper of our adolescence or not, Marcia *did* really say things like "My knees didn't get anywhere near Davy Jones," and Carol and Mike *did* drink so much coffee in the pre-decaf era that we suspected them of being closet speedfreaks. Greg's hair turned orange. Details like these can take on a surrealistic feel if you let them. In the end, *Bradymania!* is the story of a show that's funny on purpose in some places, funny without meaning to be in others, and usually capable of appealing to something we recognize in ourselves. It's not real life. It's "The Brady Bunch." And that's okay.

Henry Kissinger and two unidentified moppets
(State Department employees?) prove that the
Nixon Administration wasn't *all* bad.

PART ONE

Here's The Story

In Heaven, It's Always
Friday Night at Eight

THE CHARACTERS

MIKE BRADY

NAME:	Michael Paul Brady
A.K.A.:	Mike "Hotlips," according to a former high school girlfriend
MARITAL STATUS:	One-time widower. Had a hunch and married a lovely lady, Carol Martin
CHILDREN:	Has three boys of his own: Greg, Peter and Bobby
EDUCATION:	Fremont High School (got suspended for a week for stealing a rival high school's mascot) Norton College
OCCUPATION:	Architect
HOBBIES:	Golf Fishing and camping Ukulele Reconstructing the previous day's events Road trips

Mike Brady

FAVORITE ACTIVITIES:	Working on plans in his den Taking a coffee break with Carol Lecturing the kids
CLUBS:	Frontier Scout Council Master, Troop 2
ACHIEVEMENTS:	Chosen Father Of The Year (as a result of a composition Marcia wrote) Designed the Brady house Helped build the kids' clubhouse Built the Brady dunking booth Designed sets for the backyard production of "Snow White" Almost designed a factory for Beebe Gallini Designed a low-cost housing development Designed Don Drysdale's house Designed something in Maine Designed a house for Mrs. Foster Oversaw the construction of a building in Hawaii Designed plans for an addition to King's Island Amusement Park Designed plans to enlarge Sam's butcher shop Wrote a speech entitled, "The Use of Ancient Architecture in Modern Buildings" Designed the Penelope Fletcher Cultural Center Designed a building for a classified government project Was the master of ceremonies for a banquet in Mr. Phillips's honor
PERSONAL PREFERENCES:	Payphones Permed hair Coffee—he likes it "black and with a smile."
FAVORITE SAYINGS:	"I think you have some explaining to do." "I believe you owe us an explanation." "You have a lot of explaining to do." "I think we all learned a valuable lesson from this."

CAROL BRADY

NAME: Carol Ann Tyler
Martin Brady

A.K.A.: "Twinkles,"
according to
Tank Gates,
a former
high school
boyfriend

MARITAL STATUS: Ambiguous, but
eventually married
a man named Brady who had
three boys of his own.

CHILDREN: Three lovely girls: Marcia, Jan, and Cindy

EDUCATION: Westdale High School
State University, where they lost 35 straight
football games, according to Mike

OCCUPATION: Housewife
Freelance writer

HOBBIES: Needlepoint and sewing
Soloist in church choir
Sculpting
Photography

**FAVORITE
ACTIVITIES:** Stirring something in the kitchen
Handing out the kids' lunchbags
Having a cup of coffee with Mike
Working on a needlepoint project
Shopping

Carol Brady

CLUBS:	Anti-smoking committee
	Head of the Save Woodland Park Committee
	PTA
	Women's Club
	Chairwoman of Fillmore Junior High Play
	Committee
ACHIEVEMENTS:	Third place in sculpture contest
	Had an article published in *Tomorrow's Woman*
	magazine
	Once won a twist contest
PERSONAL	
PREFERENCES:	Pantsuits
	"O Come, All Ye Faithful"
	Coffee
	Shag haircuts
	Sculptures of horses
	Biodegradable Safe Soap

GREG BRADY

NAME: Greg Brady

A.K.A.: Johnny Bravo;
The Casanova of
Clinton Avenue
(according to
Alice)

EDUCATION: Fillmore
Junior High
School;
Westdale
High School (graduated 1974); will either
attend Norton College or State U.

HOBBIES: Girls
Guitar
Songwriting
Bike maintenance
Super 8 movies
Camping
Cars
Car Sport magazine
Surfing

SCHOOL ACTIVITIES: Student Body President
Editor of the yearbook
Member of the School Committee for 3 semesters
Frontier Scout, Troop 2
Pitcher for Pony League baseball team
Little League "Rockets" baseball team, #1
Football, #23, Westdale
Second string on Westdale's basketball team
Westdale's official photographer
Head of the Cheerleading Judging Committee
Did a rendition of "The Day Is Done" with
    Mike as part of Family Night Frolics

Greg Brady

ACHIEVEMENTS: Helped save Woodland Park
Appeared on "Hal Barton's TV Talent Review"
and "The Peter Sterne Amateur Hour"
Got the attic as his bedroom
Bought his first car for $100
Scored 94 on the driving test, 96 on the
written test
Stole Coolidge High's mascot, Raquel the
goat, and had to write a 5,000-word essay
on "The Evils of Mascot Stealing" as a
consequence.

HEROES: Don Drysdale
Wes Parker

GOAL: Rock star
Major league pitcher

PERSONAL PREFERENCES: Itching powder
Cheerleaders
Drive-ins with Rachel
Lava lamps
Hanging beads
Blue-tinted shades
Hiphuggers
White shoes or ankle-high boots
Zipper-ring shirts
Lemons, as in cars

EMPLOYMENT HISTORY: Delivery boy for Sam "after school and all
day Saturday for a buck fifty an hour"
Office assistant for Mike
Bradysitter

PETER BRADY

NAME: Peter Brady

A.K.A.: Scoop Brady
Peter The Great
Phil Packer
Canary (according
to Buddy Hinton)

EDUCATION: Fillmore Junior
High School
graduate; Westdale High School

HOBBIES: Magic
Room tapping
Bike maintenance
Camping

SCHOOL ACTIVITIES: Little League "Rockets" baseball team, #7
Offensive end on football team
Science Club
Glee Club
Drama Club (played Benedict Arnold in *George Washington*, and a palace guard in *Romeo and Juliet*)
Did a magic act for school's Old Time Vaudeville Show
Editor of "Whole Truth" column
Dumped water and feathers on Mike as part of Family Night Frolics act

ACHIEVEMENTS: Featured in *Daily Chronicle* newspaper as "Hero of the Month," as well as receiving a check for $50 and an "Outstanding Citizen" plaque for saving a girl from a falling shelf at Driscoll's Toy Shop
Awarded a lantern by Mike and Carol for *not* confessing to breaking the lamp

Peter Brady

Helped save Woodland Park
His frog, "Old Croaker," came in 35th in a
frog jumping contest
Appeared on "Hal Barton's TV Talent Review"
and "The Peter Sterne Amateur Hour"

HERO: Bobby, for saving him from a falling ladder

GOAL: To become a doctor

**PERSONAL
PREFERENCES:** Volcanoes
Old brown hats
Double-breasted leisure suits
Pork chops and applesauce
Plastic light-up skeletons

**EMPLOYMENT
HISTORY:** House detective
Jan's campaign manager for Fillmore's "Most
Popular Girl" ballot
Fired from Martinelli's Bike Shop
Fired from Haskell's Ice Cream Hut

BOBBY BRADY

NAME: Bobby Brady

A.K.A.: Shrimpo (according to Sam)

EDUCATION: Clinton Avenue Elementary School

HOBBIES: Kazoo
Drums
Bugle
Baton
Photography
Bike maintenance
Pool
Daydreaming
Checkers
Playing the organ

SCHOOL ACTIVITIES: Little League "Rockets" baseball team, #3
Cub Scouts
Little Owl
Safety monitor
Dumped water and feathers on Mike as part of Family Night Frolics act

ACHIEVEMENTS: Voted in as dues-paying mascot in Peter's Treehouse Club
Cured himself of acrophobia
Came in 4th (out of 4) in a YMCA swimming race
Attempted to break teeter-totter record
Beat Greg in chin-up contest
Almost won Golden Scoop Trophy
Awarded a trophy by his family for trying the hardest
Rescued a cat from an abandoned house

Bobby Brady

Helped save Woodland Park
Beat Mike's boss at a game of pool and won
  256 packs of gum
Schemed with Cindy to have Joe Namath visit
  him
His frog, "Spunker," came in 49th in a frog
  jumping contest
Appeared on "Hal Barton's TV Talent Review"
  and "The Peter Sterne Amateur Hour"

HEROES: Jesse James
Joe Namath

GOAL: Race car driver
Train robber
World champion pool player

**PERSONAL
PREFERENCES:** Donkey masks
Tiki idols
Skyrockets
Strawberry ice cream

**EMPLOYMENT
HISTORY:** Went bankrupt selling Neat & Natural Hair
Tonic

MARCIA BRADY

NAME: Marcia Brady

EDUCATION: Fillmore Junior High
School graduate
Westdale High School

HOBBIES: Boys
Diary maintenance
Ballet

SCHOOL ACTIVITIES: Student body
president
President of Davy Jones
Fan Club
Served on Entertainment Committee for
Fillmore's senior prom
Debating Team
Editor of *Fillmore Flyer*
Senior class president
Cheerleader
Ceramics Club
Drama Club (played Lady Capulet in *Romeo and
Juliet*)
Frontier Scout
Booster Club, Scuba Club, Karate Club, Yoga
Club, William Tell Club dropout
Did a song and dance routine to "Together
Wherever We Go" with Carol as part of
Family Night Frolics

ACHIEVEMENTS: Won "Father of the Year" essay contest
sponsored by the *Daily Chronicle* newspaper
Interviewed by a TV news reporter on Women's
Lib
Passed the Field Initiation Test for Frontier
Scout membership
Co-hostess of Senior Banquet Night

Marcia Brady

Madeover a wall flower
Earned a Daniel Boone badge, Cooking badge,
    Nature Study badge, Gypsy badge, Water
    Fun badge, and Foot Travelers badge as
    part of scout league
Awarded an "Outstanding Citizen Award" for
    something unspecified
Got Davy Jones as a date for her Fillmore
    Junior High prom
Helped save Woodland Park
Beat Greg in the obstacle course driving
    contest
Scored 98 on written driving test and 92 on
    road test (second try)
Appeared on "Hal Barton's TV Talent Review"
    and "The Peter Sterne Amateur Hour"

HERO: Desi Arnaz, Jr.

GOAL: Mrs. Desi Arnaz, Jr.
Mrs. Marcia Dentist

**PERSONAL
PREFERENCES:** Boys who collect bugs
Boys who play football
Dentists
Mini skirts
Black patent leather and platform shoes
Butterfly posters

**EMPLOYMENT
HISTORY:** Bradysitter
"Let go" from Haskell's Ice Cream Hut

JAN BRADY

NAME:	Jan Brady
A.K.A.:	Dumbhead (according to herself)
EDUCATION:	Fillmore Junior High School graduate; Westdale High School
HOBBIES:	Painting Practical jokes Reading "Teen Time Romance" magazine
SCHOOL ACTIVITIES:	Debating team Glee club Drum majorette, ballet, tap dance, drama club, and pom pom bomb-out Played a palace guard in *Romeo and Juliet*
ACHIEVEMENTS:	Voted "Most Popular Girl" Helped save Woodland Park 2nd place Honor Society Award for her essay on "Americanism: What America Means To Me" Appeared on "Hal Barton's TV Talent Review" and "The Peter Sterne Amateur Hour"
HERO:	Aunt Jenny
GOAL:	To be an only child
PERSONAL PREFERENCES:	Brunette wigs Lemons, as in fruit Sideburn banana curls Yogi Bear posters
EMPLOYMENT HISTORY:	Scooper at Haskell's Ice Cream Hut

CINDY BRADY

NAME: Cynthia Brady

A.K.A.: Cindy
Thindy

EDUCATION: Clinton Avenue
Elementary School

HOBBIES: Whining
Snooping
Tattling

SCHOOL ACTIVITIES: Glee Club
Played the Fairy Princess in the school play

ACHIEVEMENTS: Awarded a Big Jack for Best Jacks Player at
the playground
Helped save Woodland Park
Gameshow contestant on "Question The Kids"
Attempted to break teeter-totter record
Conned Joe Namath into visiting Bobby
Appeared on "Hal Barton's TV Talent Review"
and "The Peter Sterne Amateur Hour"

GOAL: To be the next Shirley Temple

**PERSONAL
PREFERENCES:** Kitty Karry-All
Pigtails

**EMPLOYMENT
HISTORY:** Magic assistant to Peter

OLIVER

NAME: Oliver (Son of Jack and Pauline, one of whom is a sibling of Carol's, although we never learn which one. He came to stay with the Bradys when his father was sent to South America to do an engineering project)

A.K.A.: The Jinx

ACHIEVEMENTS: Was the one millionth visitor to Marathon Movie Studios

EMPLOYMENT HISTORY: Assistant snoop to Cindy
Helped Bobby sell Neat & Natural Hair Tonic

HOW TO BE A JINX

Douse Greg with ketchup
Cause Bobby to break a flower pot
Unravel Carol's knitting
Cause Peter to knock over a lamp
Do something to Jan's painting
Break a vase Marcia was painting
Demolish Mike's model building

ALICE

NAME:	Alice Nelson
A.K.A.:	Sam's favorite little fillet; Sam's little lamb chop
MARITAL STATUS:	Single, never been married; Dates Sam, the butcher
EDUCATION:	Attended "either PS 34 in '43 or PS 43 in '34" Westdale High School graduate
OCCUPATION:	Live-in housekeeper
HOBBIES:	Collecting Checker Trading Stamps Soap operas Going bowling with Sam Entering contests Reading love stories Decorating Sam's apartment
ACHIEVEMENTS:	Came up with the payphone idea Won a hi-fi stereo set in the Everpressed Fabric Jingle contest Won a prize with Sam in a Charleston contest Was a contender in the Countess of Cornball competition Played Priscilla in a pilgrim festival Played John Carver in Greg's pilgrim movie Played the Wicked Queen in the Bradys' backyard production of *Snow White and The Seven Dwarfs*
GOAL:	Mrs. Sam the butcher
PERSONAL PREFERENCES:	Double-breasted blue uniforms
EMPLOYMENT HISTORY:	Waitress at the Golden Spoon Cafe at 4th and Oak

SAM

NAME:	Sam Franklin
MARITAL STATUS:	According to Alice, he's "six feet tall, two hundred pounds of unbudgeable bachelor."
OCCUPATION:	Owns a butcher shop referred to as both "Sam's Quality Meats" and "Sam's Butcher Shop"
HOBBIES:	Bowling Dating Alice Destruction derbies

ACHIEVEMENTS: Served on the Entertainment Committee for the Meatcutters Ball
Accidentally knocked out Alice's swindler boyfriend with a frozen leg of lamb
Won a prize with Alice in a Charleston contest
Made the semi-finals of the Supermarket Bowling League
Played Dopey in the Bradys' backyard production of *Snow White and The Seven Dwarfs*
While in the army, presumably, he stole the enemy code book single-handed

Sam's Quality Meats

From the counter of Sam Franklin:

Dear Alice

I lied to you. I wasn't working nights plucking chickens. I met a young woman.

At first, we just traded meatloaf recipes, then one night she asked me over to season her rump roast.

I guess I'm an old fool, but I fell for her like a pound of ground chuck!

Sam

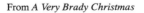

From *A Very Brady Christmas*

THE BRADYS' PETS AND ANIMALS

TIGER:	The family dog
FLUFFY:	The family cat
MYRON:	Greg's science project mouse
OLD CROAKER, SPUNKER, HERMIT, and FLASH:	Peter and Bobby's frogs
PANDORA:	The cat Bobby rescued
HENRIETTA:	Bobby's hamster
PARAKEET:	Bobby's unnamed bird
ROMEO and JULIET:	Cindy's rabbits
RAQUEL:	The goat, Coolidge High's mascot
HERMAN:	Alice's unseen goldfish
Also:	Tiger's unnamed "wife" and puppies

BRADY BUNCH FAMILY TREE

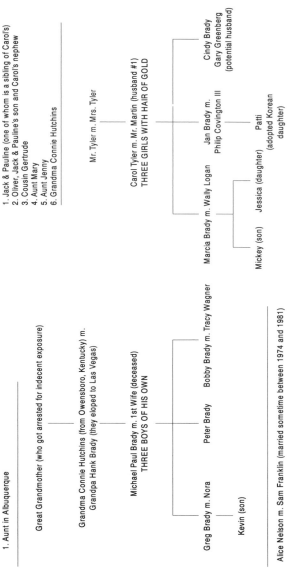

OTHER RELATIVES
1. Aunt in Albuquerque

Great Grandmother (who got arrested for indecent exposure)

Grandma Connie Hutchins (from Owensboro, Kentucky) m.
Grandpa Hank Brady (they eloped to Las Vegas)

Michael Paul Brady m. 1st Wife (deceased)
THREE BOYS OF HIS OWN

Greg Brady m. Nora   Peter Brady   Bobby Brady m. Tracy Wagner

Kevin (son)

Alice Nelson m. Sam Franklin (married sometime between 1974 and 1981)

OTHER RELATIVES
1. Emily, her older sister
2. Myrtle, her younger sister
3. Aunt Millie who gave her the strawberry recipe
4. Aunt Clara in New Mexico
5. Cousin Emma
6. Uncle Winston (dress shop owner)

OTHER RELATIVES
1. Jack & Pauline (one of whom is a sibling of Carol's)
2. Oliver, Jack & Pauline's son and Carol's nephew
3. Cousin Gertrude
4. Aunt Mary
5. Aunt Jenny
6. Grandma Connie Hutchins

Mr. Tyler m. Mrs. Tyler

Carol Tyler m. Mr. Martin (husband #1)
THREE GIRLS WITH HAIR OF GOLD

Marcia Brady m. Wally Logan   Jan Brady m.   Cindy Brady
                                      Philip Covington III   Gary Greenberg
                                                              (potential husband)

Mickey (son)   Jessica (daughter)   Patti
                                      (adopted Korean
                                       daughter)

The more things change . . .

"THE BRADY BUNCH": EPISODE SUMMARY (1969–1974)

THE BRADY BUNCH
117 half-hour shows on ABC

CREATOR AND
EXECUTIVE
PRODUCER: Sherwood Schwartz
PRODUCERS: Howard Leeds, Lloyd Schwartz
WRITERS: *(in alphabetical order)* Tom and Helen August, Gwen Bagni, William Cowley, Alan Dinehart, Paul Dubov,

As early as early Brady gets.

Herbert Finn, Ruth Brooks Flippen, Bill Freedman, Ben Gershman, Ralph Goodman, David P. Harmon, Lois Hire, Charles Hoffman, Bruce Howard, Bernie Kahn, Joel Kane, Joanna Lee, Howard Leeds, Phil Leslie, Albert E. Lewin, Jack Lloyd, Sam Locke, Michael Morris, John Fenton Murray, Howard Ostroff, Milton Pascal, Lois and Arnold Peyser, Brad Radnitz, Martin Ragaway, William Raynor, Larry Rhine, Milt Rosen, Al Schwartz, Elroy Schwartz, Sherwood Schwartz, Ray Singer, Tam Spiva, Ben Starr, Charles Stewart, Jr., Burt and Adele Styler, George Tibbles, Gene Thompson, Herb Wallerstein, Skip Webster, Paul West, Miles Wilder, Harry Winkler

DIRECTORS (in alphabetical order): Norman Abbott, David Alexander, Jack Arnold, Peter Baldwin, Allen Baron, Terry Becker, Earl Bellamy, Bruce Bilson, Ross Bowman, George Cahan, Hal Cooper, Jack Donohoe, Jerry London, Leslie H. Martinson, Russ Mayberry, Richard Michaels, Irving J. Moore, Robert Reed, John Rich, Oscar Rudolph, Lloyd Schwartz, George Tyne, Bernard Wiesen

THEME MUSIC: Frank DeVol

THEME MUSIC LYRICS: Sherwood Schwartz

THEME MUSIC SUNG BY: The Peppermint Trolley Company (first season), The Brady Kids (second through fifth season)

FIRST TELECAST: September 26, 1969 (pilot)

LAST TELECAST: March 8, 1974 (the show went into reruns through August 30, 1974)

CAST: Robert Reed . . . . Mike Brady
Florence Henderson . . . . Carol Brady
Barry Williams . . . . Greg Brady
Christopher Knight . . . . Peter Brady
Mike Lookinland . . . . Bobby Brady
Maureen McCormick . . . . . . Marcia Brady

Eve Plumb	Jan Brady
Susan Olsen	Cindy Brady
Ann B. Davis	Alice Nelson
Robbie Rist	Oliver (last six episodes)
Allan Melvin	Sam Franklin

BROADCAST
HISTORY: September 1969-September 1970, Friday, 8:00-8:30 pm
September 1970-September 1971, Friday, 7:30-8:00 pm
September 1971-August 1974, Friday, 8:00-8:30 pm

How many episodes have you seen?

Use the handy check boxes to mark the shows you've caught—and isolate the ones still out there in Rerun Land.

Bradymaniac	all 117 (including pilot)
Very Brady Fan	80–116
Groovy	40–79
Just Waiting for "The Partridge Family"	10–39
Not Clear on the Concept	0–10

PRIME TIME SCHEDULE: 1969

	7:00 PM	7:30	8:00	8:30	9:00	9:30	10:00	10:30	11:00
FRIDAY ABC		Let's Make a Deal	Brady Bunch	Mr. Deeds Goes to Town	Here Come the Brides		Jimmy Durante Presents Lennon Sisters		
CBS		Get Smart	Good Guys	Hogan's Heroes	CBS Friday Night Movie				
NBC		High Chaparal		Name of the Game			Bracken's World		

THE BRADY BUNCH
First Season (1969-1970)

(Note: Episode numbers reflect the order in which the shows were shot, not the order in which they aired.)

☐ 0. *"The Honeymoon"* (pilot). *Original airdate:* September 26, 1969. *Producer:* Sherwood Schwartz. *Writer:* Sherwood Schwartz. *Director:* John Rich. ✿ In the premiere episode, all havoc breaks loose during the

Mike and Carol share a memorable honeymoon
with the Bunch.

wedding when the boys' dog gets loose and runs after the girls' cat. When Mike and Carol miss their kids on their honeymoon, they return home to collect them. *Featuring:* J. Pat O'Malley as Mr. Tyler; Joan Tompkins as Mrs. Tyler; James Millhollin as Mr. Pringle; Dabbs Greer as the minister; Tiger; Fluffy.

☐ 1. *"Dear Libby." Original airdate:* October 3, 1969. *Producer:* Sherwood Schwartz. *Writer:* Lois Hire. *Director:* John Rich. ✿ Marcia and the rest of the kids fear that their parents' new marriage is on the rocks after she reads a letter in an advice column about a family exactly like theirs in which one of the parents is unhappy. The columnist pays a visit to the Bradys to rest their fears after receiving inquiry letters from all the kids, and Alice. Featuring: Joe de Winter as Elizabeth "Libby" Carter.

☐ 2. *"A Clubhouse Is Not a Home." Original airdate:* October 31, 1969. *Producer:* Sherwood Schwartz. *Writer:* Skip Webster. *Director:* John Rich. ✿ There's trouble in paradise. When the boys refuse to share their clubhouse with the girls, the girls decide to build their own. The boys look on and laugh, but the fun soon ends when Cindy almost gets hurt. It's togetherness one and all as the Brady men pitch in and help.

Hammer time!

☐   3. *"Kitty Karry-All Is Missing."* *Original airdate:* November 7, 1969. *Producer:* Sherwood Schwartz. *Writer:* Al Schwartz and Bill Freedman. *Director:* John Rich. ✿ Cindy accuses Bobby of stealing her favorite doll, and when Bobby's kazoo turns up missing, he points the finger at Cindy. The kids hold a trial, the jury is hung, but the mystery is soon solved. Tiger is held in contempt of court. *Featuring:* Pitt Herbert as Mr. Driscoll; Tiger.

☐   4. *"Katchoo."* *Original airdate:* October 24, 1969. *Producer:* Sherwood Schwartz. *Writer:* William Cowley. *Director:* John Rich. ✿ Jan develops an allergy, and after testing flowers, flour, and Mike, the bunch narrows it down to Tiger, whom they each secretly bathe in the hope of keeping him in the family. The case is solved when it is discovered that she's allergic to Tiger's flea powder. *Featuring:* Tiger.

☐   5. *"Eenie, Meenie, Mommy, Daddy."* *Original airdate:* October 10, 1969. *Producer:* Sherwood Schwartz. *Writer:* Joanna Lee. *Director:* John Rich. ✿ Because of a lack of space in the school auditorium, Cindy is forced to choose between inviting her mother or her father to the school play. A special provision is made and a private performance is held for the whole Brady bunch. *Featuring:* Marjorie Stapp as Mrs. Engstrom; Tracy Reed as Miss Sherry Marlowe; Brian Forster as the elf.

☐   6. *"Alice Doesn't Live Here Anymore."* *Original airdate:* October 17, 1969. *Producer:* Sherwood Schwartz. *Writer:* Paul West. *Director:* John Rich. ✿ Alice plans to leave after feeling left out and no longer needed when the boys start going to their new stepmother for help. A plan is devised and the Bunch goes out of their way to make Alice feel important and wanted. *Featuring:* Fred Pinkard as Mr. Stokey.

☐   7. *"Father of the Year."* *Original airdate:* January 2, 1970. *Producer:* Sherwood Schwartz. *Writer:* Skip Webster. *Director:* George Cahan. ✿ Marcia nominates Mike as Father Of The Year in an essay to the newspaper. When she sneaks out in the middle of the night to mail it, she gets caught and is grounded. The decision is reversed for good cause when the newspaper's publisher and photographer show up at the Bradys' to present Mike with the award. *Featuring:* Oliver McGowan as Hamilton Samuels; Bill Mullikin as Lance Pierce; Lee Corrigan as the cameraman; Bob Golden as Mr. Fields.

☐   8. *"The Grass Is Always Greener."* *Original airdate:* March 13, 1970. *Producer:* Sherwood Schwartz. *Writer:* David P. Harmon. *Director:* George Cahan. ✿ Mike and Carol learn that the grass isn't always greener when they switch roles for the day. While Carol plays baseball with the boys, Mike gives the girls a cooking lesson. The results on both sides are disastrous.

☐   9. *"Sorry, Right Number."* *Original airdate:* November 21, 1969. *Producer:* Sherwood Schwartz. *Writer:* Ruth Brooks Flippen. *Director:* George Cahan. ✿ Discussions, eggtimers and threats didn't solve the phone problem, so Mike installs a payphone to teach the kids the value of money. When Mike's phone is tied up and he's forced to use the payphone, he almost loses a deal when he runs out of time—and change. *Featuring:* Allan Melvin as Sam Franklin; Howard Culver as Mr. Crawford.

☐   10. *"Is There a Doctor in the House?"* *Original airdate:* December 26, 1969. *Producer:* Sherwood Schwartz. *Writer:* Ruth Brooks Flippen. *Director:* Oscar Rudolph. ✿ When all six kids come down with the measles, Carol calls the girls' doctor, a woman, and Mike calls the boys' doctor, a man. A dilemma develops over whose doctor to use, and it is decided that each side of the family will continue using its own doctor. *Featuring:* Marion Ross as Dr. Porter; Herbert Anderson as Dr. Cameron.

☐   11. *"54-40 and Fight."* *Original airdate:* January 9, 1970. *Producer:* Sherwood Schwartz. *Writer:* Burt Styler. *Director:* Oscar Rudolph. ✿ The Checker Trading Stamp company is going out of business and a battle ensues over who inherits Alice's trading stamps. It's the girls vs. the boys, winner-takes-all, in the fall of the house of cards game. Tiger knocks over Bobby, the house falls, and the girls go shopping—and come back with a color television set! *Featuring:* Herb Vigran as Harry; Tiger.

☐ 12. *"A-Camping We Will Go."* *Original airdate:* November 14, 1969. *Producer:* Sherwood Schwartz. *Writers:* Herbert Finn and Alan Dinehart. *Director:* Oscar Rudolph. ✿ The girls go camping for the first time ever and the boys don't want them along. After a day of fishing with no fish caught, the boys are forced to eat food brought from home.

☐ 13. *"Vote for Brady."* *Original airdate:* December 12, 1969. *Producer:* Sherwood Schwartz. *Writer:* Elroy Schwartz. *Director:* David Alexander. ✿ Marcia and Greg run against each other for student body president, and when the campaign carries over into the Brady house, the kids take sides. In an act of goodwill, Marcia bows out of the race. *Featuring:* Martin Ashe as Mr. Dickens; Stephen Liss as Rusty; Casey Morgan as Scott.

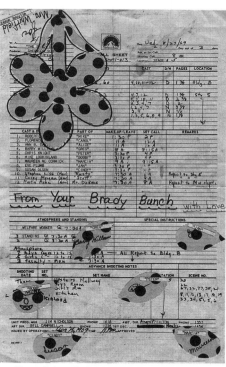

The call sheet for "Vote for Brady," decorated by the cast members

☐ 14. *"Every Boy Does It Once."* *Original airdate:* December 5, 1969. *Producer:* Sherwood Schwartz. *Writers:* Lois and Arnold Peyser. *Director:* Oscar Rudolph. ✿ After Bobby watches "Cinderella" and is asked to sweep out the fireplace by Carol, he decides to run away, convinced that Carol is going to be a wicked stepmother. He decides to stay when Carol says she'll go with him. *Featuring:* Michael Lerner as Johnny; Larry McCormick as the TV announcer; Tiger.

☐ 15. *"The Voice of Christmas."* *Original airdate:* December 19, 1969. *Producer:* Sherwood Schwartz. *Writer:* John Fenton Murray. *Director:*

Beebe Gallini seeks to have her way with Mike.

Oscar Rudolph. ✿ Carol develops laryngitis and Cindy asks a department store Santa Claus to give her her voice back so she can sing for the Christmas church services. Her wish is granted, and it's off to the church. *Featuring:* Hal Smith as Santa Claus; Carl Albert as the little boy.

☐ 16. *"Mike's Horror-Scope."* *Original airdate:* January 16, 1970. *Producer:* Sherwood Schwartz. *Writer:* Ruth Brooks Flippen. *Director:* Oscar Rudolph. ✿ The day after Carol reads Mike's horoscope about a strange woman entering his life, Mike is hired by a beautiful and exotic cosmetics entrepreneur to design her a new factory. When she visits the Brady household, Mike loses the deal when a runaway toy airplane accidentally hits his new boss and she is caught in squirtgun fire. *Featuring:* Abbe Lane as Beebe Gallini; Joe Ross as Duane Cartwright.

☐ 17. *"The Undergraduate."* *Original airdate:* January 23, 1970. *Producer:* Sherwood Schwartz. *Writer:* David P. Harmon. *Director:* Oscar Rudolph. ✿ Greg's schoolwork suffers when he develops a crush on a girl named Linda, whom everyone thinks is the new girl at school. When Mike is called in to meet Greg's math teacher, he realizes that *she* is the Linda Greg is enamored with. The situation is resolved when Dodger first baseman Wes Parker, who is engaged to the teacher, promises him tickets to opening day if his grades improve. *Featuring:* Gigi Perreau as Miss Linda O'Hara; Teresa Warder as Linda; Wes Parker as himself.

☐ 18. *"To Move or Not to Move."* *Original airdate:* March 6, 1970. *Producer:* Sherwood Schwartz. *Writer:* Paul West. *Director:* Oscar

Rudolph. ✿ Mike decides to sell the house after constant complaints about the lack of room. The kids, however, change their minds and "haunt" the house to scare away prospective buyers. *Featuring:* Fran Ryan as Mrs. Hunsaker; Lindsay Workman as Bertram Grossman.

Cindy and Bobby get busted pulling the haunted house routine.

☐ 19. *"Tiger! Tiger!" Original airdate:* January 30, 1970. *Producer:* Sherwood Schwartz. *Writer:* Elroy Schwartz. *Director:* Herb Wallerstein. ✿ Bobby fears the worst when Tiger is missing. The kids pitch in and buy an ad offering reward money to bring their beloved pet back. Tiger is found several blocks away looking after a new family of his own. *Featuring:* Maggie Malooly as Mrs. Simpson; Gary Grimes as the teenage boy; Tiger; Mrs. Tiger.

☐ 20. *"Brace Yourself." Original airdate:* February 13, 1970. *Producer:* Sherwood Schwartz. *Writer:* Brad Radnitz. *Director:* Oscar Rudolph. ✿ Marcia gets braces and is convinced that she is ugly and will go unnoticed after a boy breaks a date to take her to the school dance. The date is back on when she learns her escort had the same fears. *Featuring:* Molly Dodd as the saleslady; Mike Robertson as Craig; John Daniels as Eddie; Brian Nash as Joey; Jerry Levreau as Harold.

Beauty is in the eye . . .

☐ 21. *"The Big Sprain." Original airdate:* February 6, 1970. *Producer:* Sherwood Schwartz. *Writer:* Tam Spiva. *Director:* Russ Mayberry. ✿ Carol leaves Mike and Alice in charge when she leaves to take care of a sick aunt. The house is in chaos after Alice sprains her ankle when she slips on Chinese Checkers and Mike and the kids are left to do the household chores. *Featuring:* Allan Melvin as Sam Franklin.

☐ 22. *"The Hero." Original airdate:* February 20, 1970. *Producer:* Sherwood Schwartz. *Writer:* Elroy Schwartz. *Director:* Oscar Rudolph. ✿ Peter's head swells after he is featured as "Hero Of The Month" in the newspaper for saving a girl's life in Driscoll's Toy Shop. He is humbled when he realizes the ill effects of his attitude. *Featuring:* Pitt Herbert as Mr. Driscoll; Dani Nolan as Mrs. Spencer; Dave Morick as Earl Hopkins; Joe Conley as the deliveryman; Randy Lane as Steve; Iler Rasmussen as Jason; Susan Joyce as Jennifer; Melanie Baker as Tina Spencer.

☐ 23. *"Lost Locket, Found Locket." Original airdate:* March 20, 1970. *Producer:* Sherwood Schwartz. *Writer:* Charles Hoffman. *Director:* Norman Abbott. ✿ Jan receives a locket from a secret admirer, and when it turns up missing, the family reconstructs the previous night's events to recover it. Meanwhile, Mike and Carol each suspect the other of sending it, but the real perpetrator, Alice, is caught by Jan. *Featuring:* Jack Griffin as the guard.

☐ 24. *"The Possible Dream." Original airdate:* February 27, 1970. *Producer:* Sherwood Schwartz. *Writers:* Al Schwartz and Bill Freedman. *Director:* Oscar Rudolph. ✿ Cindy accidentally gives away Marcia's diary, in which Marcia has written about her deep feelings toward Desi Arnaz, Jr. The family scours the city's used book stores to find it, and Marcia is visited by Desi himself. *Featuring:* Desi Arnaz, Jr. as himself; Gordon Jump as Collins; Jonathan Hole as Thackery; Pat Patterson as the collection man.

PRIME TIME SCHEDULE: 1970

FRIDAY

7:00 PM	7:30	8:00	8:30	9:00	9:30	10:00	10:30
ABC	Brady Bunch	Nanny and the Professor	Partridge Family	That Girl	Love American Style	This is Tom Jones	
CBS	The Interns		The Headmaster	CBS Friday Night Movie			
NBC	High Chaparal		Name of the Game			Bracken's World	

11:00

THE BRADY BUNCH
Second Season (1970-1971)

(Note: Episode numbers reflect the order in which the shows were shot, not the order in which they aired.)

☐ 25. *"Going, Going . . . Steady." Original airdate:* October 23, 1970. *Producer:* Howard Leeds. *Writer:* David P. Harmon. *Director:* Oscar Rudolph. ✿ Marcia falls head-over-heels for a boy who is more interested in bugs than romance. The family helps her win his attention when she takes up the study of insects, but regrets it when they decide to go steady. *Featuring:* Billy Corcoran as Harvey Klinger; Rory Stevens as Lester.

☐ 26. *"The Dropout." Original airdate:* September 25, 1970 (season premiere). *Producer:* Howard Leeds. *Writers:* Ben Gershman and Bill Freedman. *Director:* Peter Baldwin. ✿ When Don Drysdale picks up architectural plans at the Brady house, he encourages Greg to become a major-league pitcher. Greg's grades suffer as a result of his obsession, and the Brady household is driven crazy by his overconfidence. He is soon put back into study mode when Don stresses the importance of an education.

Dodger ace Don Drysdale pays a visit.

The long arm of the law.

Featuring: Don Drysdale as himself.

☐ 27. *"The Babysitters."* *Original airdate:* October 2, 1970. *Producer:* Howard Leeds. *Writer:* Bruce Howard. *Director:* Oscar Rudolph. ✿ Mike and Carol hire Greg and Marcia to babysit the kids when they get last-minute tickets to a play and Alice is unavailable. Worried that something might go wrong, Mike, Carol, and Alice all head home to sneak a peek and are picked up by the cops, who are responding to a call from the kids. *Featuring:* Gil Stuart as the restaurant captain; Jerry Jones as the police officer.

☐ 28. *"The Treasure of Sierra Avenue."* *Original airdate:* November 6, 1970. *Producer:* Howard Leeds. *Writers:* Gwen Bagni and Paul Dubov. *Director:* Oscar Rudolph. ✿ While the boys are out playing ball in an empty lot, Bobby finds a lost wallet containing $1,100. The girls want their share, and when the boys say no, the girls give them the silent treatment. Mike convinces the kids to put an ad in the paper, and the wallet is claimed. *Featuring:* Victor Killian as Mr. Stoner.

☐ 29. *"The Un-Underground Movie."* *Original airdate:* October 16, 1970. *Producer:* Howard Leeds. *Writer:* Albert E. Lewin. *Director:* Jack Arnold. ✿ Greg makes a Pilgrim movie for a

Trading cards commemorate episode #29, "The Un-Underground Movie."

class project and decides to cast his family, but things get out of hand when the kids fight over their roles and Mike makes too many suggestions on his script. Greg takes charge and the film is in the can. *Featuring:* Robert Reed, Florence Henderson and Maureen McCormick as Pilgrims; Christopher Knight and Mike Lookinland as friendly Indians; Eve Plumb as Priscilla; Ann B. Davis as John Carver.

Family affair: Robert Reed's daughter Carolyn Reed (far left) and Florence Henderson's daughter Barbara Henderson (far right) guest star in "The Slumber Caper."

☐ 30. *"The Slumber Caper." Original airdate:* October 9, 1970. *Producer:* Howard Leeds. *Writer:* Tam Spiva. *Director:* Oscar Rudolph. ✿ Marcia's slumber party is canceled when her principal calls her folks to inform them of an unflattering picture she drew of her teacher. Mike and Carol accept Marcia's testimonial and the party is back on. Later, one of Marcia's friends is found to be the culprit. *Featuring:* E.G. Marshall as J.P. Randolph; Chris Charney as Paula; Hope Sherwood as Jenny; Barbara Henderson as Ruthie; Carolyn Reed as Karen.

☐ 31. *"Confessions, Confessions." Original airdate:* December 18, 1970. *Producer:* Howard Leeds. *Writer:* Brad Radnitz. *Director:* Russ Mayberry. ✿ Mom said no playing ball in the house, but that didn't stop Peter. As a result, Carol's vase is broken, and the kids try to cover Peter so he can go camping. However, Peter gets the guilts and confesses. *Featuring:* Snag Werris as the hardware man.

☐ 32. *"The Tattle-Tale." Original airdate:* December 4, 1970. *Producer:* Howard Leeds. *Writers:* Sam Locke and Milton Pascal. *Director:* Russ Mayberry. ✿ The kids are in an uproar as a result of Cindy's tattling, and so is Alice, who had an argument with Sam because of something

Cindy misunderstood. Her tongue is soon tied when she realizes the negative results. *Featuring:* John Wheeler as the postman; Tiger.

☐ 33. *"Call Me Irresponsible."* *Original airdate:* October 30, 1970. *Producer:* Howard Leeds. *Writer:* Bruce Howard. *Director:* Hal Cooper. ✿ Mike hires Greg as an office assistant so Greg can save money to buy a car. However, Greg is fired the first day after he loses important plans at a newsstand while looking at car magazines. He is given one more chance and learns the lesson of responsibility. *Featuring:* Jack Collins as Mr. Phillips; Bob Peoples as Mr. Peterson; Annette Ferra as Randy Peterson; Barbara Morrison as the drama coach; William Benedict as the news vendor; Gordon Jump as the mechanic.

☐ 34. *"The Impractical Joker."* *Original airdate:* January 1, 1971. *Producer:* Howard Leeds. *Writer:* Burt Styler. *Director:* Oscar Rudolph. ✿ What goes around, comes around. When one of Jan's practical jokes backfires, the family searches the house for Greg's escaped mouse, which Jan had hidden and which is ultimately found in the kitchen. *Featuring:* Lennie Bremen as the exterminator; Tiger; Myron as the mouse.

All for one, one for all.

☐ 35. *"A Fistful of Reasons."* *Original airdate:* November 13, 1970. *Producer:* Howard Leeds. *Writer:* Tam Spiva. *Director:* Oscar Rudolph. ✿ When Peter tries to defend Cindy against the school's bully, he comes away with a black eye and is called a coward. Mike pays a visit to the villain's folks, and when reasoning doesn't work, teaches Peter to defend himself. In a schoolyard fight, this time Peter is the victor. *Featuring:* Russell Schulman as Buddy Hinton; Paul Sorensen as Mr. Hinton; Ceil Cabot as Mrs. Hinton.

☐ 36. *"What Goes Up . . ."* *Original airdate:* December 11, 1970. *Producer:* Howard Leeds. *Writers:* William Raynor and Myles Wilder. *Director:* Leslie H. Martinson. ❀ Peter gets his buddies to let Bobby join their treehouse club, but Bobby falls and develops acrophobia. Carol feels sorry for Bobby and buys him a pet parakeet, and when the bird escapes, Bobby's fear of heights is cured after he rescues his pet on top of the swingset. *Featuring:* Jimmy Bracken as Jimmy; Sean Kelly as Tim; Brian Tochi as Tommy; Tiger; Parakeet.

☐ 37. *"Coming-Out Party."* *Original airdate:* January 29, 1971. *Producer:* Howard Leeds. *Writer:* David P. Harmon. *Director:* Oscar Rudolph. ❀ Mike's boss invites the Bunch for an outing on his boat, but the trip is postponed after Cindy, then Carol, develop tonsillitis. *Featuring:* Jack Collins as Mr. Phillips; John Howard as Dr. Howard.

☐ 38. *"The Not-So-Ugly Duckling."* *Original airdate:* November 20, 1970. *Producer:* Howard Leeds. *Writer:* Paul West. *Director:* Irving J. Moore. ❀ When Jan's heartthrob falls for Marcia and not her, she is convinced that her freckles are the cause. To save face, she invents an imaginary boyfriend to hide her embarrassment, but the family has trouble locating him when they decide to throw Jan a party. Her worries are squelched and the boys line up after she appears in her new dress. *Featuring:* Mark Gruner as Clark Tyson; Joseph Mell as the druggist.

☐ 39. *"Tell It Like It Is."* *Original airdate:* March 26, 1971. *Producer:* Howard Leeds. *Writer:* Charles Hoffman. *Director:* Terry Becker. ❀ Carol writes an article about her family for *Tomorrow's Woman Magazine,* but it is rejected for being too realistic. When she adds more fluff, it is accepted, but the tables are again turned when the editors visit the Brady household. *Featuring:* Richard Simmons as Mr. Delafield; Jonathan Hole as Willie Witherspoon; Nora Maynard as Elaine Swann.

☐ 40. *"The Drummer Boy."* *Original airdate:* January 22, 1971. *Producer:* Howard Leeds. *Writers:* Tom and Helen August. *Director:* Oscar Rudolph. ❀ Peter gets dogged on by his football teammates when they find out that he's in the Glee Club, until Rams lineman Deacon Jones shows up at practice. Meanwhile, Bobby drives the family crazy when he takes up the drums. *Featuring:* David "Deacon" Jones as himself; Bart La Rue as the coach; Jimmy Bracken as Larry; Dennis McDougall as Freddy; Pierre Williams as Jimmy.

☐ 41. *"Where There's Smoke." Original airdate:* January 8, 1971. *Producer:* Howard Leeds. *Writer:* David P. Harmon. *Director:* Oscar Rudolph. ✿ When Greg is caught smoking by Marcia and she snitches, he promises not to do it again. However, the next day a pack of cigarettes falls out of his jacket pocket just as Carol volunteers for the Anti-Smoking Committee. Alice finally notices an unfamiliar rip in the jacket, which turns out to belong to one of Greg's friends. *Featuring:* Craig Hundley as Tommy Johnson; Marie Denn as Mrs. Johnson; Gary Marsh as Phil; Bobby Kramer as Johnny.

☐ 42. *"Will the Real Jan Brady Please Stand Up?" Original airdate:* January 15, 1971. *Producer:* Howard Leeds. *Writers:* Al Schwartz and Bill Freedman. *Director:* Peter Baldwin. ✿ Jan wants to change her image and stand out from her two blonde sisters, so she invests in a brunette wig to wear to a friend's birthday party. After some humiliation, she learns she is outstanding just the way she is. *Featuring:* Marcia Wallace as the wig saleswoman; Pamelyn Ferdin as Lucy Winters; Karen Foulkes as Margie.

Trading cards commemorate episode 42, "Will the Real Jan Brady Please Stand Up?"

☐ 43. *"Our Son, The Man." Original airdate:* February 5, 1971. *Producer:* Howard Leeds. *Writer:* Albert E. Lewin. *Director:* Jack Arnold. ✿ Greg enters high school and wants to be treated like a man, which means he's too old to room with the "kids." Mike gives up his den and Greg turns it into a groovy pad, but soon misses his brothers and moves back upstairs. *Featuring:* Julie Cobb as the girl; Chris Beaumont as the boy.

☐ 44. *"The Liberation of Marcia Brady."* *Original airdate:* February 12, 1971. *Producer:* Howard Leeds. *Writer:* Charles Hoffman. *Director:* Russ Mayberry. ✿ Marcia speaks out about Women's Lib on TV, instigating a family feud. When Marcia decides to prove that women can do whatever men can do, she joins Greg's Frontier Scout Troop and passes the initiation test. The boys retaliate and Peter sells cookies for the Sunflower Girls. *Featuring:* John Lawrence as the man; Ken Sansom as Stan Jacobsen; Ken Jones as himself.

☐ 45. *"Lights Out."* *Original airdate:* February 19, 1971. *Producer:* Howard Leeds. *Writer:* Bruce Howard. *Director:* Oscar Rudolph. ✿ Cindy freaks out after seeing a magician perform a disappearing act and won't go to sleep with the lights out. Peter hires Cindy as his magic assistant to cure her fear, but the plan backfires when Bobby plays a trick and disappears. Cindy comes through in the end and volunteers to disappear next. *Featuring:* Snag Werris as the store owner; Lindsay Workman as the school teacher; Joseph Tatner as Warren.

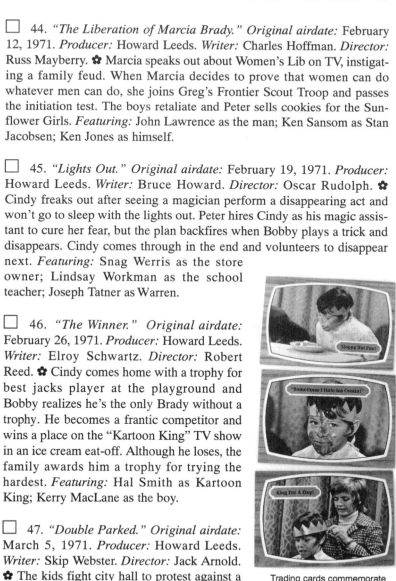

☐ 46. *"The Winner."* *Original airdate:* February 26, 1971. *Producer:* Howard Leeds. *Writer:* Elroy Schwartz. *Director:* Robert Reed. ✿ Cindy comes home with a trophy for best jacks player at the playground and Bobby realizes he's the only Brady without a trophy. He becomes a frantic competitor and wins a place on the "Kartoon King" TV show in an ice cream eat-off. Although he loses, the family awards him a trophy for trying the hardest. *Featuring:* Hal Smith as Kartoon King; Kerry MacLane as the boy.

☐ 47. *"Double Parked."* *Original airdate:* March 5, 1971. *Producer:* Howard Leeds. *Writer:* Skip Webster. *Director:* Jack Arnold. ✿ The kids fight city hall to protest against a

Trading cards commemorate episode 46, "The Winner."

courthouse being built on their parkland, and they get Carol to do the organizing. Things get hairy when Mike's firm hires him to design the new building, but the parkland is saved when his proposal for a new site is granted. *Featuring:* Jackie Coogan as the man; Jack Collins as Mr. Phillips.

☐   48. *"Alice's September Song." Original airdate:* March 12, 1971. *Producer:* Howard Leeds. *Writer:* Elroy Schwartz. *Director:* Oscar Rudolph. ✿ An old boyfriend of Alice's comes to town to court her, and when he lures her into a fraudulent proposition, the Bradys get suspicious and come to her aid. *Featuring:* Steve Dunne as Mark Millard; Allan Melvin as Sam Franklin.

PRIME TIME SCHEDULE: 1971

	7:00 PM	7:30	8:00	8:30	9:00	9:30	10:00	10:30	11:00
FRIDAY ABC			Brady Bunch	Partridge Family	Room 222	Odd Couple	Love, American Style		
CBS			Chicago Teddy Bears	O'Hara, U.S. Treasury		New CBS Friday Night Movie			
NBC			The D.A.	NBC World Premiere Movie					

THE BRADY BUNCH
Third Season (1971-1972)
(Note: Episode numbers reflect the order in which the shows were shot, not the order in which they aired.)

☐   49. *"Ghost Town, U.S.A." Original airdate:* September 17, 1971 (Season premiere). *Producer:* Howard Leeds. *Writer:* Howard Leeds. *Director:* Oscar Rudolph. ✿ This is the first in a three-part series in which the Bradys visit the Grand Canyon. In this first episode, the Bradys set up camp in Cactus Creek Ghost Town and are imprisoned by a gold prospector who thinks they've come to steal his claim. *Featuring:* Jim Backus as Zaccariah T. Brown; Hoke Howell as the gas station attendant.

☐   50. *"Grand Canyon or Bust." Original airdate:* September 24, 1971. *Producer:* Howard Leeds. *Writer:* Tam Spiva. *Director:* Oscar Rudolph.

❀ In the second of the Grand Canyon series, the Bradys break out of jail only to find that the prospector has stolen their car and trailer. Mike and Peter set out for help on foot and arrive back with their possessions and the apologetic prospector. The Bradys continue on their journey and arrive at the Grand Canyon, where Bobby and Cindy wander away from camp and get lost. *Featuring:* Jim Backus as Zaccariah T. Brown; Michele Campo as Jimmy.

The great outdoors.

☐ 51. *"The Brady Braves." Original airdate:* October 1, 1971. *Producer:* Howard Leeds. *Writer:* Tam Spiva. *Director:* Oscar Rudolph. ❀ The Bradys search for Cindy and Bobby, who are aided by a runaway Indian boy. Later, the kids bring him food, and after Mike convinces him to reunite with his tribe, the Bradys are included in the celebration and are given Indian names. *Featuring:* Jay Silverheels as Chief Dan Eagle Cloud; Michele Campo as Jimmy.

☐ 52. *"Juliet Is The Sun." Original airdate:* October 29, 1971. *Producer:* Howard Leeds. *Writer:* Brad Radnitz. *Director:* Jack Arnold. ❀ When Marcia considers turning down the lead role in the school's production of *Romeo and Juliet*, the family convinces her otherwise, and Marcia's head swells. She is humbled after losing the part and is given a smaller role. *Featuring:* Randy Case as Harold Axelrod; Lois Newman as Miss Goodwin.

☐ 53. *"The Wheeler-Dealer." Original airdate:* October 8, 1971. *Producer:* Howard Leeds. *Writers:* Bill Freedman and Ben Gershman. *Director:* Jack Arnold. ❀ Greg is talked into buying an old convertible, which

Honest Greg's used car.

turns out to be a lemon. The Bradys help him fix it up, but it's all show and no go. Greg almost pawns the clunker off on a gullible friend, but gets the guilts and sells it to the junkyard. *Featuring:* Chris Beaumont as Eddie; Charlie Martin Smith as Ronnie.

☐ 54. *"The Personality Kid."* *Original airdate:* October 22, 1971. *Producer:* Howard Leeds. *Writer:* Ben Starr. *Director:* Oscar Rudolph. ✿ Peter thinks he's dull and decides to change his personality. When he throws a party in his honor to unveil his new image, he learns that he was liked the way he was. *Featuring:* Sheri Cowart as Kathy; Monica Ramirez as Kyle; Margie De Meyer as Judy; Jay Kocen as boy #1; Pierre A. Williams as boy #2; Karen Peters as Susie.

☐ 55. *"Her Sister's Shadow."* *Original airdate:* November 19, 1971. *Producer:* Howard Leeds. *Writers:* Al Schwartz and Phil Leslie. From a story by Al Schwartz and Ray Singer. *Director:* Russ Mayberry. ✿ Jan sets out to prove herself after constantly being compared to Marcia by her teachers. When she tries out for the pom-pom team she fails to be picked; however, she receives an award by the Honor Society for an essay she wrote. After retotaling the points she realizes a mistake has been made, and wins a more valuable

Marcia. Marcia, Marcia, Marcia.

award for honorably forfeiting her glory. *Featuring:* Lindsay Workman as the principal; Gwen Van Dam as Mrs. Watson; Peggy Doyle as the teacher; Nancy Gillette as the pom-pom girl; Julie Reese as Katy.

☐ 56. *"The Teeter-Totter Caper."* *Original airdate:* December 31, 1971. *Producer:* Howard Leeds. *Writers:* Joel Kane and Jack Lloyd. *Director:* Russ Mayberry. ✿ Bobby and Cindy feel they are not important when they are told they can't attend a relative's wedding with the rest of the family. To prove their importance, they set out to break the teeter-totter record. Although they win media attention, they fail at their attempt. *Featuring:* Dick Winslow as Winters.

Alice gets dunked in episode #57, "My Sister, Benedict Arnold."

☐ 57. *"My Sister, Benedict Arnold."* *Original airdate:* October 15, 1971. *Producer:* Howard Leeds. *Writer:* Elroy Schwartz. *Director:* Hal Cooper. ✿ Marcia is asked out by a high school boy who is Greg's arch rival after beating Greg out on the first-string basketball team. After the date, Marcia isn't impressed but continues to see the boy after Greg orders her not to. Greg retaliates and dates Marcia's rival, and when things come to a boil, Mike and Carol step in to mediate. *Featuring:* Gary Rist as Warren Mulaney; Sheri Cowart as Kathy.

☐ 58. *"The Private Ear."* *Original airdate:* November 12, 1971. *Producer:* Howard Leeds. *Writer:* Michael Morris. *Director:* Hal Cooper. ✿
Peter uses Mike's tape recorder to eavesdrop on conversations, which causes the family to feud when he starts dropping comments. Marcia and Greg get suspicious and plan revenge: Peter thinks an imaginary surprise party is being thrown for him after hearing a rehearsed conversation between his siblings. Turnabout is fair play when Mike and Carol catch on, and the party's on!

☐ 59. *"And Now, a Word from Our Sponsor."* *Original airdate:* November 5, 1971. *Producer:* Howard Leeds. *Writer:* Albert E. Lewin. *Director:* Peter Baldwin. ✿ The Bradys are discovered in a supermarket parking lot and asked to star in a laundry soap commercial. However, Mike won't give his consent until the soap outcleans their current detergent. The commercial falls through after the Bradys take acting lessons from a friend. *Featuring:* Paul Winchell as Skip Farnum; Bonnie Boland as Myrna; Art Lewis as Felder; Lennie Bremen as the truck driver.

☐ 60. *"Click."* *Original airdate:* November 26, 1971. *Producer:* Howard Leeds. *Writers:* Tom and Helen August. *Director:* Oscar Rudolph. ✿ Carol doesn't approve of Greg's going out for the football team, and her fears are realized when Greg cracks a rib during practice. Greg leaves the team to become the official photographer and captures a bad call on film. *Featuring:* Elvera Roussel as Linette Carter; Bart LaRue as the coach.

☐ 61. *"The Not-So-Rose-Colored Glasses."* *Original airdate:* December 24, 1971. *Producer:* Howard Leeds. *Writer:* Bruce Howard. *Director:* Leslie H. Martinson. ✿ Mike arranges to have the kids' picture taken as an anniversary gift to Carol, but the framed picture is destroyed when Jan accidentally runs into it with her bike. The photo is retaken behind Mike's back, but he notices the difference: Jan is wearing her new glasses. Jan confesses and is almost punished, but Mike learns she sold her bike to pay for the second photo. *Featuring:* Robert Nadder as Mr. Gaylord.

☐ 62. *"Big Little Man."* *Original airdate:* January 7, 1972. *Producer:* Howard Leeds. *Writer:* Skip Webster. *Director:* Robert Reed. ✿ Discouraged because he's so small, Bobby wants to prove he's a lot bigger than his size and attempts to stretch himself by hanging from the swingset. When this proves futile, he tries to become a mental giant and nearly drives the family crazy. *Featuring:* Allan Melvin as Sam Franklin.

☐ 63. *"Getting Davy Jones."* *Original airdate:* December 10, 1971. *Producer:* Howard Leeds. *Writers:* Phil Leslie and Al Schwartz. *Director:* Oscar Rudolph. ✿ Davy Jones is in town and Marcia, president of the Davy Jones Fan Club, hastily promises to get him to sing at her prom. After several unsuccessful attempts to meet him she sneaks into a recording session. Davy overhears her plea, and the show is on! *Featuring:* David Jones as himself; Britt Leach as the manager; Marcia Wallace as Mrs. Robbins; Kimberly Beck as Laura; Tina Andrews as Doreen; Whitney Rydbeck as Page.

"How about the flip side?"

When Davy Jones reprised his role in the stage version of "Getting Davy Jones," he sported the very same jacket he wore in the episode's final scene. Yes, it still fit.

☐ 64. *"Dough Re Mi."* *Original airdate:* January 14, 1972. *Producer:* Howard Leeds. *Writer:* Ben Starr. *Director:* Allen Baron. ✿ Greg, an aspiring songwriter, is short the $150 needed to cut a record, so Peter suggests the kids combine their money and talent to record the sure-to-be hit. When Peter's voice changes, the plans are almost ruined, until Greg writes another song to accommodate his brother. *Featuring:* John Wheeler as Mr. Dimsdale.

☐ 65. *"The Big Bet."* *Original airdate:* January 28, 1972. *Producer:* Howard Leeds. *Writer:* Elroy Schwartz. *Director:* Earl Bellamy. ✿ Bobby bets Greg he can't do twice as many chin-ups as he, Bobby, can, and exercises fiercely to prove it, while Greg does nothing. As the loser, Greg has to do everything Bobby asks for a whole week, including taking him along on a date. *Featuring:* Hope Sherwood as Rachel.

☐ 66. *"Jan's Aunt Jenny."* *Original airdate:* January 21, 1972. *Producer:* Howard Leeds. *Writer:* Michael Morris. *Director:* Hal Cooper. ✿ Jan finds an old picture of her Aunt Jenny at her age and discovers they look exactly alike. Excited to meet her look-alike, Jan writes her and receives a current photo depicting an old, eccentric woman. Paranoid she'll become her aunt in later years, Jan is hesitant to greet her, but quickly learns that beauty is within. *Featuring:* Imogene Coca as Aunt Jenny.

☐ 67. *"Cindy Brady, Lady."* *Original airdate:* February 18, 1972. *Producer:* Howard Leeds. *Writers:* Al Schwartz and Larry Rhine. *Director:* Hal Cooper. ✿ Cindy is bothered about being the youngest, so Bobby becomes a secret admirer to make her feel special. Bobby gets in a bind when Cindy becomes anxious to meet him and he bribes his friend Tommy to be the admirer. Cindy catches on after other family members get the same idea, but the day is saved when Tommy admits his genuine affection for Cindy. *Featuring:* Eric Shea as Tommy Jamison.

☐ 68. *"The Power of the Press."* *Original airdate:* February 4, 1972. *Producer:* Howard Leeds. *Writers:* Ben Gershman and Bill Freedman. *Director:* Jack Arnold. ✿ Peter writes a column for the school newspaper and becomes popular with his classmates when they find their names in the paper. Trying to improve a poor grade, Peter uses the power of the press and writes a flattering article about his dull teacher. A lesson is learned about manipulation, and Peter vows to work harder. *Featuring:* Milton Parsons as Mr. Price; Angela Satterwhite as Diane; Bobby Rhia as Harvey; Jennifer Reilly as Iris.

☐ 69. *"Sergeant Emma."* *Original airdate:* February 11, 1972. *Producer:* Howard Leeds. *Writer:* Harry Winkler. *Director:* Jack Arnold. ❀ Alice goes on vacation and gets her ex-WAC cousin to fill in. The cousin starts them immediately on a rigid schedule of exercise and orderly conduct. It doesn't take the bunch long to tire of this as they await Alice's return. *Featuring:* Ann B. Davis as Emma.

☐ 70. *"The Fender Benders."* *Original airdate:* March 10, 1972. *Producer:* Howard Leeds. *Writer:* David P. Harmon. *Director:* Allen Baron. ❀ Carol gets into a minor fender bender in a parking lot and it is agreed that each will pay their own damages. However, the other party turns up at the Brady house and presents Mike with an exaggerated bill. The Bradys go to court to dispute the charges, and win. *Featuring:* Jackie Coogan as Harry Duggan; Robert Emhardt as the judge.

☐ 71. *"My Fair Opponent."* *Original airdate:* March 3, 1972. *Producer:* Howard Leeds. *Writer:* Bernie Kahn. *Director:* Peter Baldwin. ❀ The kids at school nominate wallflower Molly Webber as Hostess of Senior Banquet Night. Marcia feels sorry for Molly and gives her a makeover to help her win, but discovers that she herself will be running against her when the other contestant drops out. *Featuring:* William Wellman, Jr. as the astronaut; Debi Storm as Molly Webber; Lindsay Workman as Mr. Watkins; Suzanne Roth as Suzanne.

PRIME TIME SCHEDULE: 1972

	7:00 PM	7:30	8:00	8:30	9:00	9:30	10:00	10:30	11:00
FRIDAY ABC			Brady Bunch	Partridge Family	Room 222	Odd Couple	Love, American Style		
CBS			Sonny & Cher Comedy Hour		CBS Friday Night Movie				
NBC			Sanford & Son	Little People	Ghost Story		Banyon		

THE BRADY BUNCH
Fourth Season (1972-1973)

(Note: Episode numbers reflect the order in which the shows were shot, not the order in which they aired.)

Watch that tiki.

☐ 72. *"Hawaii Bound."* *Original airdate:* September 22, 1972 (Season premiere). *Producer:* Howard Leeds. *Writer:* Tam Spiva. *Director:* Jack Arnold. ✿ In the first of the three parts, Mike takes the family to Hawaii when his company sends him to check the construction on a building he designed. While exploring the island, Bobby finds an ancient tiki idol and learns of its tabu. *Featuring:* Don Ho as himself; David "Lippy" Espinda as Hanalei; Dennis M. Chun as the young workman; Elithe Aguiar as the hula instructor; Patrick Adiarte as David.

☐ 73. *"Pass The Tabu."* *Original airdate:* September 29, 1972. *Producer:* Howard Leeds. *Writer:* Tam Spiva. *Director:* Jack Arnold. ✿ In the second Hawaii episode, bad luck plagues the Bradys. Greg crashes while surfing, a wall-hanging almost hits Bobby and a tarantula climbs on Peter. The boys decide to return the idol to the ancient burial grounds to rid themselves of the curse. *Featuring:* David "Lippy" Espinda as Hanalei; Cris Callow as Mandy; Patrick Adiarte as David; Vincent Price as Professor Hubert Whitehead.

☐ 74. *"The Tiki Caves."* *Original airdate:* October 6, 1972. *Producer:* Howard Leeds. *Writer:* Tam Spiva. *Director:* Jack Arnold. ✿ In the last of the Hawaii episodes, the boys come across an eccentric archaeologist in the burial caves who holds them prisoner, thinking they've come to steal his find. Meanwhile, Mike and Carol set out looking for the boys after they don't return to the hotel. They catch up with them at the caves when they discover a trail of popcorn left by Bobby. *Featuring:* Vincent Price as Professor Hubert Whitehead; David "Lippy" Espinda as Hanalei; Leon Lontoc as the mayor's representative.

☐ 75. *"Today I Am a Freshman."* *Original airdate:* October 13, 1972. *Producer:* Howard Leeds. *Writers:* William Raynor and Myles Wilder. *Director:* Hal Cooper. ✿ Marcia gets the jitters on her first day of high school and stays at home. Greg introduces her to his friends, and when Marcia makes a fool of herself, she takes her folks' advice to be herself and get involved in school activities. *Featuring:* John Howard as the doctor; Vickie Cos as Kim; Kelly Flynn as Tom; John Reilly as Dick.

☐ 76. *"Cyrano de Brady."* *Original airdate:* November 20, 1972. *Producer:* Howard Leeds. *Writer:* Skip Webster. *Director:* Hal Cooper. ✿ Peter develops a crush on Jan's new girlfriend, Kerry, and enlists Greg to help win her attention after his own efforts fail. Greg plays Cyrano for Peter, but the plan backfires when Kerry catches on and rejects Peter for Greg. Greg sets out to prove he's a rat-fink by disguising Marcia as the "other woman." *Featuring:* Kym Karath as Kerry.

☐ 77. *"Fright Night."* *Original airdate:* October 27, 1972. *Producer:* Howard Leeds. *Writer:* Brad Radnitz. *Director:* Jerry London. ✿ After the boys spook the girls one night, manufacturing a ghost and eerie noises, the girls get even. They win a bet that their brothers can't spend the night in the attic after they manufacture a ghost of their own. The kids get together and try to spook Alice, which results in catastrophe when she accidentally mistakes a sculpture of Mike for a thief.

☐ 78. *"Career Fever."* *Original airdate:* November 17, 1972. *Producer:* Howard Leeds. *Writers:* Burt and Adele Styler. *Director:* Jerry London. ✿ Greg writes a school paper entitled, "The Importance Of Choosing A Career," in which, for lack of a better idea, he says he plans to become an architect. After Mike reads it, Greg doesn't have the heart to tell him the truth, so he tries to demonstrate his lack of talent. This results in Mike buying him a set of drafting tools. Greg finally confesses.

☐ 79. *"Law and Disorder." Original airdate:* January 12, 1973. *Producer:* Howard Leeds. *Writer:* Elroy Schwartz. *Director:* Hal Cooper. ✿ Appointed the school Safety Monitor, Bobby becomes unpopular when he writes up his friends for minor offenses and even more unpopular when he turns in his brothers and sisters. Bobby breaks a rule and learns his lesson when he ruins his good suit after rescuing a cat from an abandoned house. *Featuring:* Shawn Schepps as Jill; Harlen Carraher as Steve; Cindy Henderson as the girl; Jon Hayes as Jon.

☐ 80. *"Jan, the Only Child." Original airdate:* November 10, 1972. *Producer:* Howard Leeds. *Writers:* Al Schwartz and Ralph Goodman. *Director:* Roger Duchowney. ✿ Frustrated with having no privacy or identity among her siblings, Jan wishes to become an only child. The kids oblige and give Jan her space, but when she doesn't appreciate their ef-

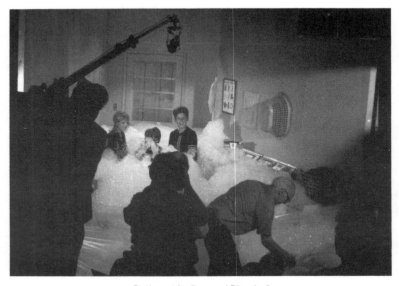

On the set for "Law and Disorder."

forts, they exclude her from their activities. Jan gets lonely, changes her mind, and rejoins the family in time to participate in the charity hoe-down.

☐ 81. *"The Show Must Go On??" Original airdate:* November 3, 1972. *Producer:* Howard Leeds. *Writer:* Harry Winkler. *Director:* Jack Donohue. ✿ Marcia talks Carol into participating in the school's "Family Night Frolics," a parent-child variety show, and when she agrees, Greg gets Mike in on it with an act of their own. Carol and Marcia do a rendition of "Together Wherever We

Greg and Mike get the feather treatment at the Family Night Frolics.

Go" and Greg accompanies Mike's reading of "The Day Is Done." *Featuring:* Allan Melvin as Sam Franklin; Barbara Morrison as Mrs. Tuttle; Brandy Carson as the woman; Karen Foulkes as Muriel; Frank De Vol as the father; Bonnie Ludeka as the daughter.

☐ 82. *"You Can't Win 'Em All." Original airdate:* March 16, 1973. *Producer:* Howard Leeds. *Writer:* Lois Hire. *Director:* Jack Donohue. ✿ Cindy and Bobby win an opportunity to become contestants on "Quiz The Kids," and while Cindy fervently prepares for the exam and wins a place, Bobby does nothing and is not selected. Cindy develops an ego about her upcoming TV appearance, but when the time comes, she blanks out when the TV light goes on. *Featuring:* Edward Knight as Monty Marshall; Vicki Schreck as a Woodside girl; Claudio Martinez as a Woodside boy; Tracey M. Lee as a Woodside girl; Harlen Carraher as a Clinton boy; Miyoshi Williams as a Clinton girl.

☐   83. *"Goodbye, Alice, Hello."* *Original airdate:* November 24, 1972. *Producer:* Howard Leeds. *Writer:* Milt Rosen. *Director:* George Tyne. ✿ Peter believes Alice intentionally squealed on him after he broke Carol's lamp, and after a couple of other miscommunications, Alice decides to leave the Bradys. The kids seek her out at the Golden Spoon Cafe, where she has taken a job as a waitress. *Featuring:* Mary Treen as Kay; Snag Werris as Mr. Foster; Harry G. Crigger as the customer.

☐   84. *"Love and the Older Man."* *Original airdate:* January 5, 1973. *Producer:* Howard Leeds. *Writer:* Martin A. Ragaway. *Director:* George Tyne. ✿ Marcia develops a crush on the family's new dentist, and she misinterprets his interest in her as a babysitter for the beginning of a romantic relationship. When Jan informs Marcia that Mr. Right is married, she sets out to break the date and is embarrassed. *Featuring:* Don Brit Reid as Dr. Stanley Vogel; Allen Joseph as the minister.

☐   85. *"Everyone Can't Be George Washington."* *Original airdate:* December 22, 1972. *Producer:* Howard Leeds. *Writers:* Sam Locke and Milton Pascal. *Director:* Richard Michaels. ✿ Peter auditions for the role of George Washington in the school play, but ends up playing Benedict Arnold when the teacher tells him he would be better suited for the more difficult role. The kids at school tease him for being Arnold the "traitor," which results in Peter trying to get himself kicked out of the play. *Featuring:* Sara Seegar as Miss Bailey; Barbara Bernstein as Peggy; Sean Kelly as Stuart; Jimmy Bracken as Freddie; Michael Barbera as Harvey; Cheryl Beth Jacobs as Edith; Angela B. Satterwhite as Donna.

☐   86. *"Greg's Triangle."* *Original airdate:* December 8, 1972. *Producer:* Howard Leeds. *Writers:* Bill Freedman and Ben Gershman. *Director:* Richard Michaels. ✿ Greg is head of the Cheerleading Judging Committee and gets in a bind when he has to choose between his new girlfriend, Jennifer Nichols, and Marcia. The situation gets worse when he has to cast the deciding vote to break the tiebreaker. Both girls lose out to a noticeably outstanding candidate. *Featuring:* Tannis G. Montgomery as Jennifer Nichols; Rita Wilson as Pat Conroy.

☐ 87. *"Bobby's Hero." Original airdate:* February 2, 1973. *Producer:* Howard Leeds. *Writer:* Michael Morris. *Director:* Leslie H. Martinson. ✿ Bobby's parents are called in by the school principal where they learn Bobby has been terrorizing his classmates while pretending to be his hero, Jesse James. After a discussion about the villain fails, Mike sets out to expose Bobby to the truth and rounds up a relative of a victim killed by James. *Featuring:* Richard Carlyle as Mr. Hillary; Burt Mustin as Jethroe Collins; Gordon De Vol as Jesse James; Ruth Anson as Miss Perry.

☐ 88. *"The Great Earring Caper." Original airdate:* March 2, 1973. *Producer:* Howard Leeds. *Writers:* Larry Rhine and Al Schwartz. *Director:* Leslie H. Martinson. ✿ Cindy loses a pair of Carol's earrings, which had been lent to Marcia, and hires Peter to find them before they are noticed missing. The earrings are found in the washing machine when the family reconstructs the events leading up to the crime.

☐ 89. *"Greg Gets Grounded." Original airdate:* January 19, 1973. *Producer:* Howard Leeds. *Writer:* Elroy Schwartz. *Director:* Jack Arnold. ✿ Greg loses his car privileges for a week when Mike and Carol learn that he almost got into a car accident while reading an album cover on the road. Greg gets in more trouble when he gets caught driving a friend's car, claiming his folks said only that he couldn't use *their* car. Life becomes unbearable when he is forced to live by exact words until he has learned his lesson. *Featuring:* Gracia Lee as Jenny; Hope Sherwood as Rachel.

☐ 90. *"The Subject Was Noses." Original airdate:* February 9, 1973. *Producer:* Howard Leeds. *Writers:* Al Schwartz and Larry Rhine. *Director:* Jack Arnold. ✿ Marcia breaks a date with "nice boy" Charley when Doug Simpson, the high school's Big Man On Campus, asks her out. However, Doug dumps her when he sees the swollen nose Marcia acquires when she is accidentally hit by a football. Marcia learns

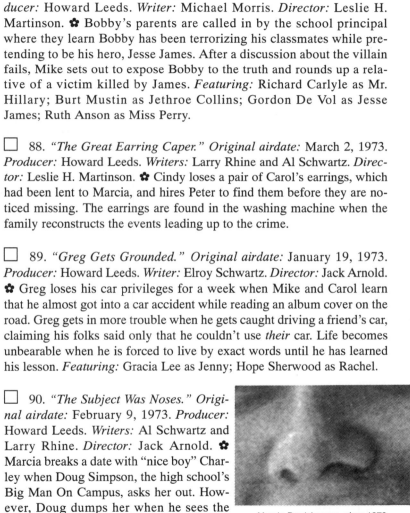

Marcia Brady's nose, circa 1973, before the accident. Is this all Doug Simpson was after?

the lesson of beauty within and apologizes to Charley. *Featuring:* Nicholas Hammond as Doug Simpson; Stuart Getz as Charley; Lisa Eilbacher as Vicki.

☐ 91. *"How to Succeed in Business?"* *Original airdate:* February 23, 1973. *Producer:* Howard Leeds. *Writer:* Gene Thompson. *Director:* Robert Reed. ✿ Peter gets an after-school job in Martinelli's Bike Shop as a bicycle repairman, and while his parents think he is doing great, he's fired for working too slowly. Embarrassed to tell them the truth, he begs Martinelli to let him work for a day when Mike and Carol come in to buy a couple of bikes. *Featuring:* Jay Novello as Mr. Martinelli; Claudio Martinez as Billy; Harlen Carreher as Leon.

☐ 92. *"Amateur Nite."* *Original airdate:* January 26, 1973. *Producer:* Howard Leeds. *Writers:* Sam Locke and Milton Pascal. *Director:* Jack Arnold. ✿ The kids are short the $56.23 needed to pick up their parents' anniversary gift. They enter a local TV amateur contest to do a song and dance act with the hope of winning the $100 first prize. Although they lose, Mike and Carol see their appearance and foot the bill for their effort. *Featuring:* Harold Peary as Mr. Goodbody; Steve Dunne as Pete Sterne; Robert Nadder as Alfred Bailey.

☐ 93. *"You're Never Too Old."* *Original airdate:* March 9, 1973. *Producer:* Howard Leeds. *Writers:* Ben Gershman and Bill Freedman. *Director:* Bruce Bilson. ✿ Carol's Grandma Hutchins and Mike's Grandfather Brady come to town, and the kids try unsuccessfully to match them up. Grandma Hutchins doesn't give up on Grandpa, however, and they elope to Las Vegas. *Featuring:* Florence Henderson as Grandma Hutchins; Robert Reed as Grandpa Brady.

☐ 94. *"A Room at the Top."* *Original airdate:* March 23, 1973. *Producer:* Howard Leeds. *Writers:* William Raynor and Myles Wilder. *Director:* Lloyd Schwartz. ✿ Greg and Marcia each appeal to their parents to convert the attic into their bedroom. Greg wins out for being the oldest but forfeits the room to Marcia after he hears her heartfelt plea. Marcia relinquishes the room after she realizes she will only have to wait one more year before Greg goes off to college and the room is hers. *Featuring:* Chris Beaumont as Hank.

PRIME TIME SCHEDULE: 1973

	7:00 PM	7:30	8:00	8:30	9:00	9:30	10:00	10:30	11:00
FRIDAY ABC			Brady Bunch	Odd Couple	Room 222	Adam's Rib	Love, American Style		
CBS			Calucci's Dept.	Roll Out		CBS Friday Night Movie			
NBC			Sanford & Són	The Girl with Something Extra	Needles & Pins	Brian Keith Show	Dean Martin Show		

THE BRADY BUNCH
Fifth Season (1973-1974)
(Note: Episode numbers reflect the order in which the shows were shot, not the order in which they aired.)

☐ 95. *"Snow White and the Seven Bradys."* *Original airdate:* September 28, 1973. *Producers:* Howard Leeds and Lloyd Schwartz. *Writer:* Ben Starr. *Director:* Bruce Bilson. ♣ The Bradys put together a backyard production of "Snow White and the Seven Dwarfs" and solicit Sam and Alice to participate in the benefit to buy a retirement gift for Cindy's teacher. The show begins late when Sam and Mike head to the grocery store for an apple and are questioned by a police officer, who makes them get a permit before the play begins. *Featuring:* Frances Whitfield as the school teacher, Mrs. Whitfield; Elvenn Havard as the policeman; Allan Melvin as Sam Franklin; Florence Henderson as Snow White; Robert Reed as Prince Charming; Ann B. Davis as the Wicked Queen; Allan Melvin as Dopey; Barry Williams as Doc; Christopher Knight as Sneezy; Mike Lookinland as Bashful; Maureen McCormick as Sleepy; Eve Plumb as Happy; Susan Olsen as Grumpy.

☐ 96. *"Mail Order Hero."* *Original airdate:* September 21, 1973. *Producers:* Howard Leeds and Lloyd Schwartz. *Writer:* Martin A. Ragaway. *Director:* Bruce Bilson. ♣ Bobby lies to his friends and tells them that Joe Namath drops by the Brady house when he's in town—and gets himself into a bind when Namath is scheduled to play a game in town the fol-

Joe Namath puts the big-league hold on Bobby. Note young Brady's dignified expression.

lowing week. Cindy writes a letter to the football player begging him to grant a wish made by her dying brother to meet him. Namath shows up and Mike and Carol catch on. *Featuring:* Joe Namath as himself; Tim Herbert as Herb; Larry Michaels as Burt; Eric Woods as Tom; Kerry MacLane as Eric.

☐ 97. *"The Elopement." Original airdate:* December 7, 1973. *Producers:* Howard Leeds and Lloyd Schwartz. *Writer:* Harry Winkler. *Director:* Jerry London. ✿ Marcia and Jan overhear Alice discussing elopement with Sam and the whole family gets involved in planning a surprise wedding reception for the couple. (Actually, the two were discussing Sam's cousin Clara.) Meanwhile, Carol begins interviewing for a temporary housekeeper while the newlyweds honeymoon. When Sam and Alice show up at the reception, the Bunch learn that it was all a misunderstanding. *Featuring:* Allan Melvin as Sam Franklin; Byron Webster as the Reverend; Bella Bruck as Gladys.

☐ 98. *"Adios, Johnny Bravo." Original airdate:* September 14, 1973 (Season premiere). *Producers:* Howard Leeds and Lloyd Schwartz. *Writer:* Joanna Lee. *Director:* Jerry London. ✿ When the kids audition for a TV amateur show, Greg is spotted by an agent, who wants to sign him on as the new Johnny Bravo. Greg has visions of super-

The old song and dance.

stardom and decides to drop his college plans, until he learns he was hired because he fit the costume, not for his talent. *Featuring:* Claudia Jennings as Tami Cutler; Paul Cavonis as Buddy Berkman; Jeff Davis as Hal Barton.

☐ 99. *"Never Too Young."* *Original airdate:* October 5, 1973. *Producers:* Howard Leeds and Lloyd Schwartz. *Writers:* Al Schwartz and Larry Rhine. *Director:* Richard Michaels. ❀ Bobby discovers girls after he is kissed by Millicent for having defended her at school. However, Millicent later informs Bobby that she may have the mumps, and Bobby fears that he may have quarantined his family from a big Roaring Twenties party. It's a false alarm, and the party's on. *Featuring:* Melissa Anderson as Millicent.

Mike and Carol prepare to start a flap.

☐ 100. *"Peter and the Wolf."* *Original airdate:* October 12, 1973. *Producers:* Howard Leeds and Lloyd Schwartz. *Writer:* Tam Spiva. *Director:* Leslie H. Martinson. ❀ Greg's Friday night date with Sandra is in jeopardy when her cousin Linda comes to visit. He can't get any of his friends to risk a blind date, so he enlists the help of Peter, who disguises himself as an older man. The date's a disaster, and the girls get even with Greg at an Italian restaurant where Mike and Carol are entertaining some clients in an-

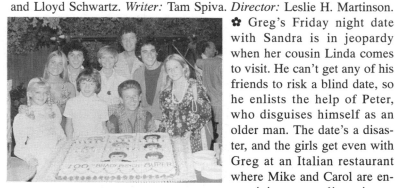
The cast celebrates its 100th episode.

Here's the story
    It's time to tell it —
It's about us kids they call
            THE BRADY BUNCH —
For the last five years
    we've worked and played together
And even eaten lunch!
It's the story
    of growing older
And becoming known and liked
        from coast to coast —
Mom and Dad and Alice, too,
    delight the people
Who tune us in the most —
Now it's time to stop
    and look both ways and listen
And we hope to hear renewal
        coming thru —.
But these years we'll always cherish
        and remember
And we'll, also, always love
        THE BUNCH OF YOU —
THE BUNCH OF YOU — THE BUNCH OF YOU —
That's the way we feel about
        THE BUNCH OF YOU!

A touching poem from the kids to the rest of the cast and crew. Despite the optimistic line about "renewal coming through," there was to be no sixth season.

other booth. *Featuring:* Christopher Knight as Phil Packer; Cindi Crosby as Sandra Carter; Kathie Gibboney as Linda; Paul Fierro as Mr. Calderon; Alma Beltran as Mrs. Calderon; Bill Miller as Len.

☐ 101. *"Getting Greg's Goat."* *Original airdate:* October 19, 1973. *Producers:* Howard Leeds and Lloyd Schwartz. *Writers:* Milton Pascal and Sam Locke. *Director:* Robert Reed. ✿ Greg steals the rival high school's mascot, a goat, and hides it in his attic room. The family believes he's hiding a girl, and when Mike heads up to talk to his son, he learns the truth. Greg has a hard time getting the goat out of the house and is caught with the evidence by Carol's PTA group taking a tour of the house. *Featuring:* George D. Wallace as Mr. Binkley; Sandra Gould as Mrs. Gould; Margarita Cordova as the 1st PTA lady; Selma Archerd as the 2nd PTA lady.

☐ 102. *"The Cincinnati Kids."* *Original airdate:* November 23, 1973. *Producers:* Howard Leeds and Lloyd Schwartz. *Writers:* Al Schwartz and Larry Rhine. *Director:* Leslie H. Martinson. ✿ The kids are invited to accompany Mike to King's Island Amusement Park in Cincinnati, Ohio, where Mike is scheduled to deliver plans on expanding the

Just a little off the top, please.

park. While the kids enjoy the rides, Mike learns that his plans have been accidentally switched for a Yogi Bear poster bought by Jan. When Jan is found and admits she lost the other poster tube, a frantic and ultimately successful search begins. *Featuring:* Hilary Thompson as

Those darned plans.

Marge; Bob Hoffman as the attendant; L. Jeffrey Schwartz as the Bear.

☐ 103. *"Quarterback Sneak." Original airdate:* November 9, 1973. *Producers:* Howard Leeds and Lloyd Schwartz. *Writers:* Ben Gershman and Bill Freedman. *Director:* Peter Baldwin. ✿ A quarterback from the rival high school feigns romantic interest in Marcia in order to sneak a peek at Greg's football playbook. Marcia is finally convinced of his intentions after her brothers set up a mock playbook and he is caught in the act. Mike catches on and makes Greg tell the culprit about the scheme—but Greg's suspicious opponent refuses to believe the confession and loses

Accidents will happen.

the game as a result. *Featuring:* Denny Miller as Tank Gates; Chris Beaumont as Jerry Rogers; Don Carter as Rich.

☐ 104. *"Marcia Gets Creamed." Original airdate:* October 26, 1973. *Producers:* Howard Leeds and Lloyd Schwartz. *Writers:* Ben Gershman and Bill Freedman. *Director:*

Peter Baldwin. ✿ Marcia gets a part-time job at Haskell's Ice Cream Hut, which annoys her boyfriend because she no longer has time for him. Marcia gets Peter a job so that she will have more time—and ends up firing him because he goofs off. Jan takes his place, and the tables turn when Marcia is let go by the owner in favor of her more enthusiastic sister. *Featuring:* Henry Corden as Mr. Haskell; Michael Gray as Jeff; Kimberly Beck as the girl.

☐ 105. *"My Brother's Keeper." Original airdate:* November 2, 1973. *Producers:* Howard Leeds and Lloyd Schwartz. *Writer:* Michael Morris. *Director:* Ross Bowman. ✿ Bobby saves Peter from being hit by a falling ladder in their backyard, and Peter promises to become Bobby's slave for life, insisting on doing anything the younger boy wishes. Bobby takes advantage of the situation, and Peter's enthusiasm soon wears out.

☐ 106. *"Try, Try Again." Original airdate:* November 16, 1973. *Producers:* Howard Leeds and Lloyd Schwartz. *Writers:* Al Schwartz and Larry Rhine. *Director:* George Tyne. ✿ After bombing out in ballet, Jan takes up tap dancing, but when she practices at home the Bunch lose their patience. Peter encourages her to try out for the school play, where she auditions for the part of an artist. Although she fails again, the teacher recognizes her artistic talent. *Featuring:* Judy Landon as Miss Clairette; Ruth Anson as Mrs. Ferguson; Darryl Seman as Billy Naylor.

The old soft shoe with Kelly's kids.

☐ 107. *"Kelly's Kids." Original airdate:* January 4, 1974. *Producers:* Howard Leeds and Lloyd Schwartz. *Writer:* Sherwood Schwartz. *Director:* Richard Michaels. ✿ In this pilot for a possible new series, the Bradys' new neighbors, the Kellys, decide to adopt eight-year-old Matthew from an orphanage, and when Matt misses his pals, Dwayne and Steve, they are also adopted, despite their racial diversity. Matt overhears his new mother discussing an unapproving neighbor, and the three boys run away to the Brady house. *Featuring:* Ken Berry as Ken Kelly; Brooke Bundy as Kathy Kelly; Todd Lookinland as Matt; William Attmore II as Dwayne; Carey Wong as Steve; Jackie Joseph as Miss Phillips; Molly Dodd as Mrs. Payne.

☐ 108. *"The Driver's Seat."* *Original airdate:* January 11, 1974. *Producers:* Howard Leeds and Lloyd Schwartz. *Writer:* George Tibbles. *Director:* Jack Arnold. ✿ Marcia bets Greg that she can score higher on her driver's test but flakes out when she gets behind the wheel. Meanwhile, Jan, who is also having a problem appearing before an audience, uses some advice of Mike's. Marcia also takes the tip and passes, but learns that their scores are even. Mike sets up an obstacle course for the two to maneuver, and Greg gets over-anxious and loses. *Featuring:* Herb Vigran as the examiner.

☐ 109. *"Miss Popularity."* *Original airdate:* December 21, 1973. *Producers:* Howard Leeds and Lloyd Schwartz. *Writer:* Martin Ragaway. *Director:* Jack Donohue. ✿ Jan is nominated as the Most Popular Girl in her class, and the family pitches in to help her campaign and win. However, Jan gets herself in trouble looking for votes when she makes promises she can't keep to her classmates. She realizes her wrongdoing when she begins to lose friends, and sets out to right her wrongs. *Featuring:* Darryl Seman as Herman; Jerelyn Fields as Shirley.

☐ 110. *"Out of this World."* *Original airdate:* January 18, 1974. *Producers:* Howard Leeds and Lloyd Schwartz. *Writers:* Al Schwartz and Larry Rhine. *Director:* Peter Baldwin. ✿ After Bobby and Peter meet real-life astronaut James McDivitt, who reports having seen a UFO while in space, they camp out in their backyard to spot one of their own. Convinced one night that they have made a sighting, they borrow Carol's camera to capture it on film. Greg confesses that he manufactured the spaceship after they take the evidence to an expert. *Featuring:* Brigadier General James A. McDivitt as himself; Mario Machado as himself; James

Close encounters of the Brady kind.

Flavin as Police Captain McGregor; Frank Delfino as Herlo the Kaplutian; Sadie Delfino as Shim the Kaplutian.

☐ 111. *"Two Petes in a Pod." Original airdate:* February 8, 1974. *Producers:* Howard Leeds and Lloyd Schwartz. *Writers:* Sam Locke and Milton Pascal. *Director:* Richard Michaels. ✿ Peter learns that he has a look-alike at school. He takes advantage of the situation when his double agrees to go on a blind date with Mike's boss's niece so Peter can go out with a girl he made a date with for the same night. Mike and Carol catch on, but all ends well when the niece admits she's having a good time with the impostor Peter. *Featuring:* Christopher Knight as Arthur Owens; Robbie Rist as Cousin Oliver; Denise Nickerson as Pamela; Kathy O'Dare as Michelle.

☐ 112. *"Welcome Aboard." Original airdate:* January 25, 1974. *Producers:* Howard Leeds and Lloyd Schwartz. *Writers:* Larry Rhine and Al Schwartz. *Director:* Richard Michaels. ✿ Carol's kid

The Bunch—plus Oliver, minus Mike—at Marathon Studios.

nephew Oliver is set to stay for the summer; he soon believes he's a jinx after several accidents occur while he is around. His fear is relieved when he is numbered the one-millionth visitor to the Marathon Movie Studios, and the entire Bunch appears in a zany western movie. *Featuring:* Robbie Rist as Cousin Oliver; John Nolan as Mr. Douglas; Judd Laurance as the director; Snag Werris as the Keystone Kop; Dick Winslow as truck driver #1; Ralph Montgomery as truck driver #2; Lloyd Schwartz as the slate clapper.

☐ 113. *"The Snooperstar."* *Original airdate:* February 22, 1974. *Producers:* Howard Leeds and Lloyd Schwartz. *Writer:* Harry Winkler. *Director:* Bruce Bilson. ❀ To cure her sister of snooping, Marcia baits Cindy with an entry in her diary about a talent scout coming to discover her as the next Shirley Temple. When a difficult client of Mike's appears at the Brady household, Cindy thinks this is the talent agent and puts on her best performance. Cindy saves Mike's account when she wins the affection of his client—and learns a lesson about minding her own business. *Featuring:* Natalie Schafer as Penelope Fletcher; Robbie Rist as Cousin Oliver.

☐ 114. *"The Hustler."* *Original airdate:* March 1, 1974. *Producers:* Howard Leeds and Lloyd Schwartz. *Writers:* Bill Freedman and Ben Gershman. *Director:* Michael Kane. ❀ Mike's boss sends him a pool table, and Bobby soon develops a talent for the game. Dreaming about being the next great pool shark, he even beats Mike's boss when he's invited over to dinner one night. However, Mike gives the pool table to charity after admitting they have no room for it in their house. *Featuring:* Robbie Rist as Cousin Oliver; Jim Backus as Mr. Harry Matthews; Dorothy Shay as Frances Matthews; Charles Stewart as Joe Sinclair; Leonard Bremen as the truck driver; Jason Dunn as Hank Thompson; Susan Quick as Gloria Thompson; Grayce Spence as Muriel Sinclair.

☐ 115. *"Top Secret."* *Original airdate:* February 15, 1974. *Producers:* Howard Leeds and Lloyd Schwartz. *Writer:* Howard Ostroff. *Director:* Bernard Wiesen. ❀ The boys believe that Mike is working on secret plans after an FBI agent visits the Brady house. When Sam asks Mike for help on a confidential project, they get the idea he intends to pass on the plans to the Russians. In an effort to save their country, they lock Sam in his meat locker and hold him prisoner. It is soon learned that Sam's confidential project is nothing more than plans to enlarge his butcher shop. *Featuring:* Robbie Rist as Cousin Oliver; Allan Melvin as Sam Franklin; Lew Palter as Mr. Gronsky; Don Fenwick as Fred Sanders.

A scene from the show's final episode.

☐ 116. *"The Hair-Brained Scheme."* *Original airdate:* March 8, 1974. *Producers:* Howard Leeds and Lloyd Schwartz. *Writer:* Charles Stewart, Jr. *Director:* Jack Arnold. ✿ Bobby is determined to make a million dollars selling Neat & Natural Hair Tonic and sells his first bottle to Greg. Unfortunately, the product flunks the test when Greg's hair turns orange and he is forced to dye his hair to its natural color in time for his high school graduation. *Featuring:* Robbie Rist as Cousin Oliver; Bern Hoffman as the first man; John Wheeler as the second man; Brandy Carson as the woman; Hope Sherwood as Gretchen; Barbara Bernstein as Suzanne.

Near the end of the series.

THE CAST, THEN AND NOW

ROBERT REED (1932-1992)

> "I should have tried to get out of the show, rather than inflict my views on [the cast]." — To *People* magazine.

Robert Reed
circa 1967 . . .

. . . 1977 . . .

. . . and 1987.

Anxious for his big break, Robert Reed thought he had finally made it when he auditioned for a couple of Warner Brothers westerns, "The Lawman" and "Maverick." After all, he'd been a real cowboy in real life, having grown up on his father's 3,000-acre mink ranch in Oklahoma. Despite this qualification, the casting director turned him down.

Robert Reed was born John Robert Rietz in Highland Park, Illinois, on October 19, 1932. He never legally changed his name from Rietz to Reed, probably because he didn't like his stage name: "I think of vanilla pudding or tapioca when I think of Reed," he once said.

The Rietz family moved to Muskogee, Oklahoma, when he was six. As a child he was a farm boy: he raised award-winning show calves, belonged to the 4-H Club, and rode a school bus twenty-five miles to the nearest school. It was in high school that Robert first became interested in acting, joining the drama club. He also played basketball and participated in the debating program. At sixteen he received an award from the National Forensic Society. At seventeen he was writing and producing for local radio stations, and even worked as an announcer.

Upon graduation Robert enrolled at Northwestern University as a drama major. He continued his studies at the Royal Academy of Dramatic Arts in London, taking his new wife, fellow Northwestern student Marilyn Rosenberg, with him. Although his marriage lasted only a couple of years, they produced a daughter, Carolyn, who just recently had a child of her own.

When Robert returned to the United States, he joined an off-Broadway company called The Shakespearewrights, playing leading roles in *Romeo and Juliet* and *A Midsummer Night's Dream*. In 1956 he became a member of Chicago's Studebaker Theater, where he met E.G. Marshall (later his co-star in "The Defenders").

Robert relocated to Hollywood and appeared in TV shows like "The Lawman," "The Danny Thomas Show," and "Men Into Space." The turning point came in 1959 when he played an attorney on "Father Knows Best." This led directly to the Emmy-winning "The Defenders." He also appeared on Broadway in Neil Simon's *Barefoot In The Park*, replacing Robert Redford, and in the original company of Richard Rodgers's *Avanti!*

As part of Paramount's stable of contract players, Robert tested for three pilots, and was ultimately cast as the father in "The Brady Bunch," a part he was unenthusiastic about. He was a method actor, a dramatic actor, not suited for the "gags and gimmicks" of "The Brady Bunch," as he once said. Nevertheless, he liked the Bunch enough to take them on an all-expense paid trip to London aboard the QE2 during the show's heyday.

Concurrent with "The Brady Bunch," Robert had a recurring role as Lieutenant Adam Tobias in "Mannix."

Robert received Emmy nominations for his performances in two mini-series, "Rich Man, Poor Man" and "Roots," and for his portrayal of a transsexual doctor in "Medical Center."

He continued his theatre work and appeared on such TV shows as "Murder, She Wrote" and "Highway To Heaven." Robert also taught a course in Shakespearian acting.

He died in May of 1992 in Pasadena, California; an autopsy indicated that he had contracted the AIDS virus.

❀   ❀   ❀

Spotlight on Robert Reed

Favorite episode: "To be honest, I don't have a favorite. The locations were all fun, though—Hawaii, Grand Canyon, and the amusement park in Cincinnati."

To what do you attribute the success of "The Brady Bunch?"
"Making the kids identifiable to their peer groups. These kids were real enough and had real enough problems for other kids to identify with. The humor that was written was gentle humor. Today's comedy is very mean spirited, one-liner to one-liner, usually at the expense of others."

Reaction to the pilot, "The Honeymoon" (to TV Guide, 1970):
"The pilot turned out to be 'Gilligan's Island' with kids . . . Sherwood is a compulsive rewriter; and as an old gag man, what he writes is gags. I can always tell what he has put into a script—it's like riding along a smooth concrete highway and then hitting a rough spot of asphalt."

On "The Brady Bunch" (to *People* magazine, May 1992): "It was just as inconsequential as can be. To the degree that it serves as a baby-sitter, I'm glad we did it. But I do not want it on my tombstone."

(Unless otherwise noted, above quotes are courtesy of writer Max Merlin.)

❀   ❀   ❀

Robert Reed's Credits

AS A REGULAR

"The Defenders," CBS, 1961-1965; "The Brady Bunch," ABC, 1969-1974; "Mannix," CBS, 1969-1975; "The Brady Bunch Hour," ABC, 1977;

"The Runaways," NBC, 1978; "Nurse," CBS, 1981-1982; "The Bradys," CBS, 1990.

TV SERIES (selected) "The Danny Thomas Show," CBS, 1959; "Father Knows Best," CBS, 1959; "The Lawman," ABC, 1959; "Men Into Space," CBS, 1960; "Dr. Kildare," NBC, 1963-1965, several appearances; "Family Affair," CBS, 1966; "Ironside," NBC, 1967; "Love American Style," ABC, 1969 & 1971 2 appearances; "The Mod Squad," ABC, 1972; "Mission Impossible," CBS, 1972; "Harry O," ABC, 1974; "McCloud," NBC, 1975; "Medical Center," CBS, 1975; "The Streets Of San Francisco," ABC, 1976; "Barnaby Jones," CBS, 1977; "The Love Boat," ABC, 1977-1985 several appearances; "Vega$," ABC, 1978 & 1979, 2 appearances; "Fantasy Island," ABC, 1978 & 1983, 2 appearances; "Galactica 1980," ABC, 1980; "Charlie's Angels," ABC, 1980; "Hotel," ABC, 1983 & 1984, 2 appearances; "Murder, She Wrote," CBS, 1985 & 1988 2 appearances; "Duet," Fox, 1987; "Hunter," NBC, 1987; "Jake and the Fatman," CBS, 1987; "Snoops," CBS, 1989; "Day By Day," NBC, 1989, as Mike Brady; "Free Spirit," ABC, 1989, (with Florence Henderson); "Jake and the Fatman," CBS, 1992.

INFOMERCIALS "Consumer Resource Institute Weight Loss and Control Subliminal Tapes," 1989; "Cellular Telephone," 1992.

TV MOVIES, MINI-SERIES AND SPECIALS (selected) "The City," ABC, 1971; "The Man Who Could Talk To Kids," ABC, 1973; "Rich Man, Poor Man," ABC, 1976; "The Boy In The Plastic Bubble," ABC, 1976; "The Brady Bunch Variety Hour," ABC, 1976; "Roots," ABC, 1977; "SST-Death

Flight," ABC, 1977; "Scruples," CBS, 1980; "Casino," ABC, 1980; "The Brady Girls Get Married," NBC, 1981; "Death Of A Centerfold: The Dorothy Stratten Story," NBC, 1981; "The ABC Afterschool Special: Between Two Loves," ABC, 1982; "International Airport," ABC, 1985; "A Very Brady Christmas," CBS, 1988.

MOVIES *The Hunters*, 1958; *Bloodlust*, 1959; *Hurry Sundown*, 1967; *Star!*, 1968; *The Maltese Bippy*, 1969.

THEATRE *A Midsummer Night's Dream*, Shakespearewrights, off-Broadway; *Romeo and Juliet*, Shakespearewrights, off-Broadway; *A Month In The Country*, Chicago Studebaker Theatre, 1956; *Barefoot In The Park*, Broadway, 1963 to 1967; *Avanti!*, Broadway, 1968; *Deathtrap*, Broadway, 1978-1982; *Alone Together*, La Mirada Civic Theatre (with Florence Henderson), 1989.

EMMY NOMINATIONS "Medical Center," actor, single performance in a drama or comedy series, 1975-1976; "Rich Man, Poor Man," supporting actor in a drama series, 1975-76; "Roots," Part 5, actor, single performance in a drama or comedy series, 1976-1977.

FLORENCE HENDERSON

> "We were in Hawaii on one of those huge outriggers and I knew that Susan couldn't swim. And the camera boat lost control, and they were coming right at us and swamped us. The next thing I knew, we were all thrown out of the boat and I was hanging upside down. I scraped all the skin on the side of my legs and all I could think of was to hang on to Susan, and I held on to her for dear life. We had no lifejackets on. And we all got back in and did [the scene] again."

In real life Florence Agnes Henderson really comes from a big bunch—in fact, an even bigger bunch than the Bradys. Born in Dale, Indiana on Valentine's Day in the midst of the Depression, Florence was the youngest of ten children. Her father Joseph was a sharecropper and was sixty-seven at her birth. Her mother Elizabeth was twenty-five years his junior.

Then.

As a child Florence milked cows, wore fifth-hand dresses, and attended Catholic school in neighboring Owensboro, Kentucky. Movies were a way to escape the harsh reality of poverty, providing hope of a better world. At home, singing was always part of her life; and by the age of two Florence had learned fifty songs, note-perfect.

Encouraged by the nuns, Florence sang for the church choir and later for the Kiwanis and the American Legion. As a senior in high school she chose the prestigious American Academy of Dramatic Arts in New York City to further her vocation. Unable to afford tuition herself, she was sponsored through the generosity of a wealthy friend.

In 1951 Florence spent a year at the Academy and landed a part in the musical *Wish You Were Here*.

Now.

Although the part was small, she caught the attention of Richard Rodgers, who cast her in the lead for the national tour of *Oklahoma!* This led to many acclaimed performances including *The Great Waltz*, *Fanny*, *The Sound of Music*, *The King and I*, and *South Pacific*.

In 1956 Florence married theatrical producer Ira Bernstein, and they started a bunch of their own: Barbara, Joseph, Robert, and Elizabeth.

But she wasn't limited to the stage. Florence became a popular variety show attraction, appearing with Ed Sullivan, Dean Martin, Bing Crosby, and Jack Paar. She broke new ground in television as the first woman to host "The Tonight Show." She was also a member of the "Today Show" team, doing weather and light news.

In 1969 Florence landed the role as Carol Brady in "The Brady Bunch." It was her first series, and she would come back to do all subsequent Brady specials and series. After "The Brady Bunch," she went on to make guest appearances in such shows as "Murder, She Wrote," "The Love Boat" and "It's Garry Shandling's Show."

For nine seasons beginning in 1985, Florence hosted her own cooking/talking show, "Country Kitchen," on The Nashville Network. Are you surprised to learn that it was sponsored by Wesson Oil? The show proved so popular that Florence put together a collection of recipes and anecdotes called *A Little Cooking, A Little Talking and A Whole Lot of Fun*. In fact, the demand has been so high that she is in the process of writing a second volume. Florence has also collaborated with Shari Lewis on another book, *One-Minute Bible Stories: New Testament*. A superb and versatile entertainer, Florence was recently named by the *Wall Street Journal* number five in a list of the top ten endorsers from the entertainment world, ranked by consumer appeal.

After twenty-five years, Florence's marriage with Ira Bernstein ended. In 1987 she married Dr. John Kappas, the founder of the Los Angeles-based Hypnosis Motivation Institute. They live in Marina del Rey, California, on a yacht once featured on the series "Lifestyles of the Rich and Famous."

Florence's charitable activities include hosting the United Cerebral Palsy Telethon and working with City of Hope, the House Ear Institute, and Childhelp USA, among others.

✿   ✿   ✿

Spotlight on Florence Henderson

Favorite performers: Sean Connery, Mary Martin, Michael Jackson, Bruce Springsteen.

The person I would have liked to meet: Clark Gable.

If I couldn't be an actor, I would be: "A full-time hypnotherapist."

First job: "Taking care of other people's children when I was still a child. Later I was a soda jerk in Rockport, Indiana, at a bus station. That was my best job."

Worst job: "Cleaning people's houses for very little money."

Favorite episode: "I loved when we got out of the studio and went to the Grand Canyon and Hawaii."

How I most resemble Carol Brady: "We are both mothers and wives and have great concern for our families."

Most frequently asked question: "Where are the children?"

Florence Henderson's Credits

AS A REGULAR "Sing Along," CBS, 1958; "The Jack Paar Show," NBC, 1958-1962 (substitute host); "Oldsmobile Music Theatre," NBC, 1959; "The Today Show," NBC, 1959-1960; "The Brady Bunch," ABC, 1969-1974; "The Brady Bunch Hour," ABC, 1977; "The Brady Brides," NBC, 1981; "Country Kitchen," The Nashville Network, 1985-present; "The Bradys," CBS, 1990; "Superfudge," ABC, 1995.

TV SERIES (selected) "The Big Record," CBS, 1958; "Car 54, Where Are You?," NBC, 1962; "The Voice of Firestone," ABC, 1958-1962 several appearances; "The Ed Sullivan Show," CBS, 1964; "I Spy," NBC, 1966; "Medical Center," CBS, 1975 & 1976, 2 appearances; "Good Heavens," ABC, 1976; "Donny & Marie," ABC, 1976; "The Love Boat," ABC, 1976-1985 several appearances; "Hart To Hart," ABC, 1981; "Police Squad," ABC, 1982; "Fantasy Island," ABC, 1982 & 1983, 2 appearances; "Alice," CBS, 1983; "Finder Of Lost Loves," ABC, 1984; "Cover Up," CBS, 1985; "The New Love American Style," ABC, 1985; "It's Garry Shandling's Show," Fox, 1988; "Murder, She Wrote," CBS; "Day By Day," NBC, 1989 (as Carol Brady); "Free Spirit," ABC, 1989 (with Robert Reed); "Dave's World," CBS, 1993-1994, recurring role; "The Mommies," NBC, 1994; "Roseanne," ABC, 1994.

Florence Henderson in a publicity still for the 1961 touring production of "The Sound of Music."

TV MOVIES, SPECIALS AND PILOTS (selected) "The Rodgers and Hammerstein Anniversary Show," 1954; "Little Women," CBS, 1958; "A Salute to Television's 25th Anniversary," ABC, 1972; "The Brady Bunch Variety Hour," ABC, 1976; "Bob Hope's All-Star Comedy Special From Australia," NBC, 1978; "The ABC After School Special: Just A Regular Kid: An

AIDS Story," ABC 1987; "A Very Brady Christmas," CBS, 1988; "Bradymania!," ABC, 1993; "Salute To The '70s," NBC, 1993; The MTV Movie Awards," MTV, 1993 (as Carol Brady); "A Tribute To Moms," E! Entertainment Television, 1994.

MOVIES *Song Of Norway*, 1970; *Shakes The Clown*, 1992; *Naked Gun 33⅓* (as herself).

THEATRE (selected) *Wish You Were Here*, Broadway debut, 1952; *Oklahoma!*, national tour, 1952; *The Great Waltz*, Los Angeles Civic Opera, 1953; *Fanny*, Broadway, 1954; *The Sound Of Music*, national tour, 1961; *The Girl Who Came To Supper*, Broadway, 1963; *The King And I*, Los Angeles Music Center, 1965; *South Pacific*, Lincoln Center, 1967; *Annie Get Your Gun*, national tour, 1974; *Bells Are Ringing*, Los Angeles Civic Light Opera, 1978-1979; *Alone Together*, La Mirada Civic Theatre (with Robert Reed), 1989.

BOOKS *One-Minute Bible Stories: New Testament* by Florence Henderson and Shari Lewis, 1986; *A Little Cooking, A Little Talking And A Whole Lot Of Fun* by Florence Henderson, 1988.

INFOMERCIALS "Kurtain Kraft."

BARRY WILLIAMS

"I remember being impressed with Maureen right away, but she was too young. I was moving fast in those days!"

Then.

BARRY WILLIAMS

Now.

From the get-go, Barry Williams was born into the Good Life. Born Barry William Blenkhorn on September 30, 1954, he was raised in Pacific Palisades, an affluent suburb of Los Angeles. His father owned a chain of credit bureaus and his mother stayed home to look after Barry and his two older brothers, Craig and Scott.

Peter Graves, then in the series "Fury," lived down the street, and although Barry was only four years old at the time, this so impressed him that he decided to pursue acting; he even told his parents so. When he was eleven he gave his parents an ultimatum and was soon enrolled in an acting class. Shortly thereafter he found an agent, Toni Kellman, who ultimately ended up representing five of the six Brady kids.

Under Kellman's direction, Barry landed the lead role in a documentary called "Why Johnny Can Read." He also did several commercials. One year later, his big break came in the series "Run For Your Life," starring Ben Gazzara (which happened to be his father's favorite show). He played a tough city snot. From there he appeared on such shows as "Dragnet," "Adam 12," "Mod Squad," "Gomer Pyle," and "That Girl." John Rich, who directed the last two shows, was set to direct the first six episodes of "The Brady Bunch." Recognizing Barry's talent, he probably played an influential role in Barry's becoming a Brady.

After "The Brady Bunch" was canceled, Barry won the lead in the road production of *Pippin*. Later he enrolled at Pepperdine University, but soon dropped out, a decision Barry regrets. Trapped somewhere between boy and man, he found subsequent roles difficult to win. A tough period followed. He found solace for a short time in drinking, supporting himself by gambling his unemployment checks.

Barry got back on track by returning to his first love: the stage. Doing mainly regional theatre, he has performed in *Oklahoma!*, *West Side Story*, *They're Playing Our Song*, *I Do! I Do!*, and *Promises, Promises*. In 1988 he bought his own ticket to New York, where he auditioned for a job as Scott Bakula's replacement in *Romance/Romance* and won. Barry is still very active in the theatre world, his most recent role being Don Quixote in *Man of La Mancha* in Palm Springs, California.

After three years of marriage to former Miss Arizona Diane Martin, Barry's marriage ended. He is now officially "auditioning" for his Juliet. Barry continues to live in the San Fernando Valley of southern California.

Currently, Barry is taking his highly successful book, (you've been in a cave if you haven't heard of it) *Growing Up Brady* on the road in a nationwide college tour.   His lecture recounts his Brady years and life in showbiz and has been such a hit that he was nominated for "Best Lecture" by Campus Activities Today.

✿   ✿   ✿

Spotlight On Barry Williams

Favorite Performer: Bette Midler

The person who I would most like to meet: "Neil Armstrong. While on the moon."

If I had more time I would: Play more tennis

If I couldn't be an actor, I would be: "A doctor or lawyer."

First job: "I was the paper route king from the time I was eight for three years."

Worst job: "Cleaning up stables, where I worked at a ranch."

Favorite Brady Bunch memory: "Being out on the beach [in Hawaii] where the local surfers were paid to make sure I got the best waves while we were filming."

Favorite episode: "The Hawaii episodes and 'Cyrano De Brady' [#76] because I liked the brotherness of it. I also liked the pilgrim show [#29, "The Un-Underground Movie"]."

Most frequently asked question: "Did you date Maureen McCormick?"

How I most resemble Greg: "I genuinely care about my Brady siblings. I tend to be responsible and protective. I'm reasonably level headed."

How I don't resemble Greg: "I was more experimental. I smoked at the time. I was the youngest in my real family life."

Barry Williams' Credits

AS A REGULAR	"General Hospital," ABC, 1969; "The Brady Bunch," ABC, 1969-1974; "The Brady Kids," ABC, 1972-1974; "The Brady Bunch Hour," ABC, 1977; "General Hospital," ABC, 1984; "The Bradys," CBS, 1990.
TV SERIES	"Here Come The Brides," ABC; "Run For Your Life," NBC; "The Andy Griffith Show," CBS; "Dragnet," NBC; "Adam 12," NBC; "It Takes A Thief," ABC; "The Invaders," ABC, 1967; "The FBI," ABC, 1968; "The Mod Squad," ABC; "Lancer," CBS, 1968; "Marcus Welby, M.D.," ABC, 1969; "That Girl," ABC; "Gomer Pyle, U.S.M.C.," CBS; "Mission Impossible," CBS,

1970; "Police Woman," NBC, 1976; "Three's Company," ABC, 1982; "Highway To Heaven," NBC; "Murder, She Wrote," CBS, 1986.

TV MOVIES, SPECIALS AND PILOTS | "The Shameful Secrets of Hastings Corners," NBC pilot, 1970; "The Brady Bunch Variety Hour," ABC, 1976; "The Brady Girls Get Married," NBC, 1981; "A Very Brady Christmas," CBS, 1988; "Bradymania!," ABC, 1993; "Salute To The '70s," NBC, 1993; "The MTV Movie Awards," MTV, 1993 (as Greg Brady).

MOVIES | *Wild In The Streets*, 1968; *Fresh Horses*, 1988; *The Brady Bunch*, 1995 (as a music producer).

THEATRE | *Pippin*, 1974-1975; *Oklahoma!*; *The Music Man*; *I Love My Wife*; *Born Yesterday*; *West Side Story*; *I Do! I Do!*; *Wait Until Dark*; *Movie Star*, Westwood Playhouse, 1982; *Promises, Promises*; *They're Playing Our Song*; *Romance/Romance*, Broadway, 1988; *City Of Angels*, 1992; *Man of La Mancha*, 1994.

BOOKS | *Growing Up Brady*, by Barry Williams with Chris Kreski, 1992 (Warner).

CHRISTOPHER KNIGHT

"We played practical jokes. In fact, we nearly made Maureen McCormick cry. There was an episode where she had to wear braces, so she had to get real ones put on for three days. We kept on telling her that they were really going to hurt and that they'd stain her teeth and push them in. She really believed us!" —to *Tigerbeat*, 1972

Then.

Now.

Being a middle child is familiar ground for Christopher Anton Knight, born on November 7, 1957, in New York City. Off-camera, he is the second-oldest of four children born to Edward and Wilma ("Willie") Knight. He has a brother, Mark, who is a year older, a sister, Lisa, who is three years younger, and another brother, David, who is seven years younger. The family relocated to southern California and finally settled in Woodland Hills.

Christopher first became interested in acting while watching his actor father perform at San Diego's Old Globe Theatre. His father would later co-own a theatre called "The Onion Company."

As with many youngsters starting out, Christopher started in commercials, graduating to shows that included "Mannix," "Gunsmoke," and "Bonanza." He also appeared in the feature film *The Narrow Chute*, starring Don Murray. Christopher's big break came with "The Brady Bunch" when he was ten years old. At the time he was attending a public junior high school. Later, because of the difficulty of balancing an actor's life and public school, he transferred to a more accommodating professional children's school.

An animal lover, Christopher had a small zoo of his own. With his brother, he raised tropical fish and award-winning racing pigeons.

Following "The Brady Bunch," Christopher appeared in a couple of made-for-TV movies, including "Diary Of A Hitchhiker" (ABC, 1979) and "Valentine Magic On Love Island" (NBC, 1980). He also guest-starred on "The Love Boat," "Happy Days," and the NBC soap opera "Another World." In 1979 he landed another series, "Joe's World," playing the son of a house painter. It was canceled after the first season. He has returned for all the Brady reunion shows.

Christopher has since removed himself from the acting arena. He worked as a casting assistant for a while, but is currently general manager of a software development company. He is separated and lives in the Los Angeles area.

✿   ✿   ✿

Spotlight on Christopher Knight

On auditioning for "The Brady Bunch": "I don't remember the interviews themselves but I do remember the incident that happened with my family after the auditions. We were down in San Diego—my dad was visiting or doing a play or something. My dad likes bargain hunting, and we went down to Tijuana and bought a bunch of clay pots. Now, there's four kids in my family and there's six of us in this little Datsun and he had bought more pots than he could take back in one trip. My mom yelled and screamed and got pissed off at him. At home, my aunt was staying with us, and for some reason she didn't have the phone number where we were in San Diego. He had to make a special trip back and called to tell her. So she told him, 'Bring Chris back, they want him for the "Brady Bunch" thing.' So I went back. If he hadn't bought those pots, I don't think that I would have been on 'The Brady Bunch.' "

Favorite episode: "Hawaii was a lot of fun, but the girls didn't have as much [work] to do as the guys. We were the ones losing the tiki and finding it and going here and there. We were there I think eleven days. We worked seven or eight of them; the girls worked three or four of them. So they had more time to have fun!' "

On "The Personality Kid" (#54): "I never realized I would coin a phrase during it—porkchops and applesauce. It's funny, because that whole thing goes back to when they wrote the show and they said there's a Humphrey Bogart impersonation. And I said, 'Who's Humphrey Bogart?' There happened to be a Humphrey Bogart movie on the night before we started shooting that episode, but I didn't watch it. I fell asleep and never knew who Humphrey Bogart was. So Lloyd [Schwartz], who was associate producer at the time, told me how to do it. So you see me doing Lloyd doing Humphrey Bogart. Little did I know how bad my impersonation was."

To what do you attribute the success of "The Brady Bunch?"
"It was because we didn't deal with any social dilemma, we only dealt with moral dilemmas. Every one of the shows had a moral, and that's very important for children. That's why every different generation can grow up in it and grow through it. Because it's teaching the same things. If I watch 'All In The Family,' it loses a little bit of its meaning because we've developed as a society."

Did you resemble Peter in real life? "Well, I'm more or less the middle child. Everybody thinks he [Peter] is real sweet, but underneath he can be a real problem. And that's the way I was as a kid, inadvertently bringing it to Peter. In other words, there's not one level . . . I think I'm getting too deep, because 'The Brady Bunch' is not multi-level. It is what it is."

What was the feeling when the show was cancelled in 1974? " I think there was the feeling that we all wanted to go off and do other things. I wasn't sure I wanted to be an actor. All my summers were spend doing 'The Brady Bunch.' I wanted to live a normal life. I wanted to go back to high school and take P.E. and science and all that other stuff, and really get to know those kids in my neighborhood who looked at me kind of odd because I was the guy who never was around, but who everyone knew. I didn't know anybody. I was dying to meet friends my own age. So I went out and developed this strategy in life where everybody's my friend. Now I have a dilemma where I don't have enough time for everybody."

(Above quotes courtesy of writer Max Merlin.)

Christopher Knight's Credits

AS A REGULAR	"The Brady Bunch," ABC, 1969-1974; "The Brady Kids," ABC, 1972-1974; "The Brady Bunch Hour," ABC, 1977; "Joe's World," NBC, 1979-1980; "Another World," NBC, 1981; "The Bradys," CBS, 1990.
TV SERIES	"Mannix," CBS; "Gunsmoke," CBS, 1968; "Bonanza," NBC; "One Day at a Time," CBS, 1976; "The Bionic Woman," NBC, 1977; "Little House on the Prairie," NBC, 1977; "CHiPs," NBC, 1978; "Happy Days," ABC, 1978; "The Love Boat," ABC, 1985; "Day By Day," NBC, 1989 (as Peter Brady).
TV MOVIES, SPECIALS AND PILOTS	"The ABC After School Special: Sara's Summer Of The Swans," (with Eve Plumb) ABC, 1974; "The Brady Bunch Variety Hour," ABC, 1976; "Diary Of A Hitchhiker," ABC, 1979; "Valentine Magic On Love Island," NBC pilot, 1980; "The Brady Girls Get Married," NBC, 1981; "A Very Brady Christmas," NBC, 1988; "Bradymania!," ABC, 1993; "Salute To The 70s," NBC, 1993; "The MTV Movie Awards," MTV, 1993 (as Peter Brady).
MOVIES	*The Narrow Chute*, 1970; *Just You And Me Kid*, 1979; *Good Girls Don't*, USA cable, 1993.
THEATER	*Letting Go*; *Accommodations*; *Mousetrap*; *Mrs. Dally Has A Lover*; *A Life In The Theater*.

MIKE LOOKINLAND

"I was the last person cast . . . it was between me and Eric Chase ('Here Come The Brides'), who had black hair. Apparently, they liked me better but I had to dye my hair. It was horrible, I hated it. For the pilot they used the darkest brown they had but because of the intensity of the lights it bled right through and my hair was red again. So for the first season they used Miss Clairol Jet Black. I remember looking at the bottle on the countertop as they were rubbing it in my hair."

Then (without dyed hair).

Then (with dyed hair).

Mike, his wife Kelly, Scott (almost four years old) and nine-month-old Joseph.

Michael Paul Lookinland, the middle child of Paul and Karen Lookinland, was born on December 19, 1960, in Mount Pleasant, Utah. His father relocated the family to the San Fernando Valley, where he was employed with the Los Angeles City School District as a teacher. Mike's mother was also a teacher, but eventually gave it up to manage her kids' careers in showbiz. Shortly thereafter the family moved again and settled in San Pedro.

Mike began his career in television at age seven after a woman who had seen a photo of Mike at his father's office suggested that his son's wholesome looks were a sure thing for commercial work. Mike got an agent and the suggestion paid off. Soon Mike was doing spots for Band-Aids and Cheerios, and he even gained recognition as the Eldon Toy boy, doing some thirty spots for them. He was offered his first series role as Eddie Corbett on "The Courtship of Eddie's Father" (ABC,1969-1972), but declined in favor of "The Brady Bunch." Concurrently, he appeared on "The Jonathan Winters Show," "Funny Face," and "The Wonderful World of Disney."

Terese, his older sister by two years, worked as a print ad model and did a few commercials as well. Todd, the youngest by four years, had a fairly successful career, appearing in such TV movies as "Guess Who's Sleeping In My Bed" (ABC, 1973), "How The West Was Won" (ABC, 1977), as well as the feature film *The Karate Kid* (1984). Todd also played Matt, the adopted son of Ken and Kathy Kelly in "The Brady Bunch" episode, "Kelly's Kids" (#107).

Besides Mike's interests in Cub scouting and the building and launching of model rockets, he sang and played the piano and organ in his family's folk singing group, performing mainly for charities.

After "The Brady Bunch" ended, Mike continued acting and won a role in the feature film *The Towering Inferno* (1974). He has since come back for all the Brady reunion shows. In "The Bradys" he fulfills Bobby's boyhood dream of becoming a race car driver, but ends up in a wheelchair after his car crashes. That's the bad news. The good news is that he marries MTV VJ Martha Quinn. Unfortunately, we never found out whether he recovers, as the series was canceled, but a hunch says he pulls through.

Mike attended the University of Utah in Salt Lake City, originally majoring in chemical engineering, but later switching into the film studies program. He left just shy of graduating when he took an opportunity to work as a production assistant for Robert Redford's Sundance Institute. Preferring to spend his time behind the camera, Mike now works freelance as a camera assistant and has been credited on such films as *A Midnight Clear*, *The Stand* and *Gambler 5*.

He and his wife Kelly, whom he married in 1988, live in Salt Lake City and have a two-year-old son, Scott. A confirmed "Deadhead," Mike has seen the Grateful Dead over one hundred times!

Spotlight on Mike Lookinland

Favorite performer: Mel Blanc

The person who I would most like to meet: "I *met* a lot of people I would have liked to meet. To me, everyone, even the most renowned scholar or rock star, is just a regular person in reality."

If I had more time I would: "I would spend more time in the back country, in the wilderness, in the as-yet-unspoiled areas of our country, getting to know it better so that what's left, stays left."

First job: "I was a hand model for a paper towel commercial. They liked me because I didn't chew my fingernails."

Worst job: "On a film called *Angel* [released as *China O'Brien*]. It was my first job as a camera assistant and I was being trained. It was horrible. People constantly saying 'You're an idiot,' 'Why can't you do anything right?' fourteen hours a day. Two cameras were going constantly and I was the only second assistant and I'd never done it before in my life. One of the special effects guys blew himself up accidentally right in front of me and died a couple of days later."

Brady Bunch memory: "Probably being on the Queen Elizabeth II . . . . On the QE II, that was the closest I had ever come to dying. The wind was close to eighty knots. You couldn't stand up and you had to hang on with all your might just not to get blown over. You weren't allowed on the deck but we [Mike, Eve, and Chris] snuck up anyway. Well, I was filming them on my super-8 camera and I took a step away from the wind screen—and all of a sudden I was sailing on the wet deck towards the side of the ship. It was a crosswind, and it was just like I was on ice skates. There was nothing I could do. I hit the rail and went over, and I remembered looking at my camera, which was attached by a wrist strap, dangling down below me. I was looking at the Atlantic ocean . . . Chris pulled me back by my pant legs."

Favorite episode: "The Pilgrim one ["The Un-Underground Movie," #29] . . . . There's ones that I don't even remember doing or even having made that, like, when I see them on TV it's like, wow, this is weird."

Least favorite episode: "I don't have a least favorite, but I had arguments with Lloyd and Sherwood about things I thought that kids my age would never do in a million years. I didn't realize at the time that all it is is comedy—it doesn't have to be real. Like when I was acting out this dog begging bit ["Amateur Night," #92]. Some of those scenes really got to me at the time, but now I don't feel that way at all."

Most frequently asked question: "Do you still get paid?" (No.)

How I resemble Bobby Brady: "He'll never grow up, and maybe I won't either. I'm working on it, though!"

How I don't resemble Bobby Brady: "The Bobby that we all know and love is eight years old. I'm thirty-two."

❁   ❁   ❁

Mike Lookinland's Credits

| AS A REGULAR | "The Brady Bunch," ABC, 1969-1974; "The Brady Kids," ABC, 1972-1974; "The Brady Bunch Hour," ABC, 1977; "The Bradys," CBS, 1990. |

| TV SERIES | "The Jonathan Winters Show," CBS, 1968; "Funny Face," CBS, 1971 (with Jodie Foster); "The Wonderful World of Disney: Dead Man's Bayou," NBC, 1971; "Day By Day," NBC, 1989 (as Bobby Brady). |

TV MOVIES, SPECIALS AND PILOTS "The Point," ABC, 1971; "Dead Men Tell No Tales," CBS, 1971; "The Brady Bunch Variety Hour," ABC, 1976; "The Brady Girls Get Married," NBC, 1981; "A Very Brady Christmas," CBS, 1988; "Salute To The 70s," NBC, 1993; "The Stand," ABC, 1994, cameo with Stephen King (Mike was also credited as second assistant cameraman).

MOVIES *The Towering Inferno*, 1974; *The Brady Bunch*, 1995 (as a police officer).

MAUREEN McCORMICK

> "(Barry Williams and I) made out in his dressing room, but we could never go too far because there always were six mothers and a social worker on the set." —to *People* magazine, 1988

Maureen Denise McCormick was born on August 5, 1956, to Richard and Irene McCormick. Her father was a public school teacher. The youngest and only daughter, Maureen has three brothers, Michael, Kevin, and Dennis.

When Maureen was six, her mother entered her in a "Baby Miss San Fernando Valley" search, and she won. It wasn't long after that she was discovered by a Hollywood talent agent. She made her acting debut in 1964 at the age of seven, winning the lead role in Ray Stark's play, *Wind It Up And It Breaks* at the La Jolla Playhouse.

Quickly progressing into commercials, Maureen garnered parts in some fifty, including spots for Kool-Aid and Kellogg's, which featured her budding singing talent. In one she was the voice of the Peanuts character Peppermint Patty. She also was selected to record the soundtracks for Chatty Cathy and the rest of Mattel's female talking dolls, about two dozen recordings in total.

Maureen broke into series television, making appearances in "Bewitched," "I Dream Of Jeannie," "My Three Sons," and "Camp Runamuck," to name a few. She also had a bit part in the 1969 Elia Kazan film *The Arrangement* (Kirk Douglas, Faye Dunaway).

Her big break, though, came when she

Then. (That's Eve Plumb in the background.)

Now.

answered a cattle call for "The Brady Bunch" and won the role of Marcia, elevating her to teen idol status. She was so popular, in fact, that she was asked to write an advice column, "Dear Maureen," for *16 Spec* magazine. One year she even won *16* magazine's Female Star of The Year Award.

After the series ended, her first role was on a "Harry O" episode, where she played a heroin addict! Following were more episodic guest stints including "Fantasy Island," "Streets of San Francisco," and "The Love Boat." Her film work includes *The Idolmaker*, *Skatetown USA*, and *Texas Lightning*, for which she wrote and sang the theme song, "It's A Typical Day."

Except for "The Bradys," Maureen came back for all the Brady reunion shows. According to Sherwood, he and the rest of the cast asked her to participate in "The Bradys" up until the day before shooting began, but she declined. Apparently Maureen wants to shed her Brady image, although that didn't stop her from appearing on a "Day By Day" episode as a very, very pregnant Marcia Brady. (If you haven't seen it, you must. A tape of this episode is a must for any serious "Brady Bunch" collector, one of the most hilarious half-hours in television sitcom history.)

Sponsored by the Upjohn Company of Kalamazoo, Michigan, Maureen is the spokeswoman for a series of birth control seminars at colleges and universities nationwide—a subject not broached on "The Brady Bunch." In fact in the last episode, "The Hair-Brained Scheme," cousin Oliver tells Cindy, "You know something, Cindy? I think your Mom has a problem discussing sex." In a nutshell!

Maureen is currently busy putting together her debut modern country album tentatively (and appropriately) titled, "Here's the Story." She also sang backup on one of Eddie Money's albums.

Maureen is married to Michael Cummings, who is employed in the computer industry. They live in the Los Angeles area and have a five-year-old daughter, Natalie.

✿   ✿   ✿

Spotlight on Maureen McCormick

On auditioning for "The Brady Bunch": "It was really fun. All I remember was that there were a ton of boys and girls. He

[Sherwood] really wanted to know what our personalities were like more than anything. He wanted to get people who were nice to work with. There were a lot of callbacks."

Favorite episode: "I guess the Hawaii episodes. It was fun to go there. The slumber party was a lot of fun, because Sherwood's daughter, Hope, was in that as well as Florence's daughter, Barbara, and we were all real close and spent a lot of time together."

To what do you attribute the success of "The Brady Bunch?"
"I think it was because of the great relationships we had with each other on the set. We became friends and it showed. It was kind of like having another family. We spent a lot of time together, even outside of the studio."

Did you resemble Marcia in real life? "Sure. I think all of us took ideas from real life."

(Above quotes courtesy of writer Max Merlin.)

✿   ✿   ✿

Maureen McCormick's Credits

AS A REGULAR	"The Brady Bunch," ABC, 1969-1974; "The Brady Kids," ABC, 1972-1974; "The Brady Bunch Hour," ABC, 1977; "The Brady Brides," NBC, 1981.
TV SERIES	"Bewitched," ABC; "The Farmer's Daughter," ABC, 1964; "I Dream of Jeannie," NBC, 1965; "Honey West," ABC, 1965; "Camp Runamuck," NBC, 1965; "My Three Sons," CBS, 1968; "Harry O," ABC, 1974; "Joe Forrester," NBC, 1975; "Westside Medical," ABC, 1977; "Nancy Drew," ABC, 1977; "Fantasy Island," ABC, 1981; "The Love Boat," ABC, 1981; "Vega$," ABC; "Lou

Grant," CBS; "The Streets of San Francisco," ABC; "The New Love American Style," ABC, 1986; "Day By Day," NBC, 1989 (as Marcia Brady); "Herman's Head," Fox, 1993.

TV MOVIES, SPECIALS, AND PILOTS "Gibbsville: The Turning Point of Jim Malloy," NBC, 1975; "The Brady Bunch Variety Hour," ABC, 1976; "A Vacation in Hell," NBC, 1979; "When, Jenny? When?," syndicated, 1980; "A Very Brady Christmas," CBS, 1988; "Faculty Lounge," pilot; "Safe At Home," cable.

MOVIES *The Boys*, 1961; *The Arrangement*, 1969; *Pony Express Rider*, 1976; *Moonshine County Express*, 1977; *Casey's Shadow*, 1978; *Take Down*, 1979; *Skatetown, USA*, 1979; *The Idolmaker*, 1980; *Texas Lightning*, 1981; *Return to Horror High*, 1987; *High School*; *That's Adequate*.

THEATRE *Wind It Up And It Breaks*, La Jolla Playhouse, 1964; *McCarthy*, Odyssey Theatre; *Peter Pan*, San Bernardino Civic Theatre.

OTHER "Here's The Story" (working title), Maureen's debut modern country album on Phantom Records. Release date set for late 1994.

EVE PLUMB

> (In answer to the question, "Which was your favorite 'Brady Bunch' episode?":) "The last one. Everyone was horrified that I was making jokes about 'The Brady Bunch.' That was a strange one—people wanting to sanctify you, for heaven's sake." — To the Chicago *Tribune*

Born on April 29, 1958, across from the Walt Disney Studios, in Burbank, Eve Plumb seems to have been predestined to go into show business. And the fact that her father, Neely, was a record producer and talent agent and her mother, Flora, a former actress and ballet teacher, didn't exactly hinder this young starlet's chances.

Like Jan, she wasn't an only child. Her older sister, Flora, also followed in the family's footsteps, graduating from UCLA's Dramatic Arts Department. Her brother Ben, however, graduated from Harvard and went on to work in South America after working in a food program in Brazil.

In 1964, at the age of six, Eve began her career doing a spot for a fabric softener commercial. She was cast in her first pilot two weeks later. After guesting in shows like "The Big Valley," "It Takes A Thief," "Mannix," and "Gunsmoke," and shooting some forty commercials, she landed the role of Jan on "The Brady Bunch."

At the time she was a ten-year-old attending Van Nuys Elementary School. Later Eve switched to a private school that was more flexible about her frequent absences.

Then.

Now.

While maintaining her status on the honor roll, both in regular school and studio school, she was a member of the Jimmy Joyce Children's Chorus and took judo, ballet, and guitar lessons. An accomplished equestrian, she won a number of awards as a show-horse rider, a hobby she became involved in while on the "Lancer" series.

After "The Brady Bunch" ended in 1974, Eve went on to become a varsity cheerleader and homecoming queen. Would we expect anything less?

Eve came out of semi-retirement in 1976, playing a teenage prostitute in the TV movie "Dawn: Portrait Of A Teenage Runaway." In 1978 she appeared in the NBC four-hour mini-series "Little Women" as Beth March. If you are familiar with Louisa May Alcott's novel, you know that Beth dies. But Eve was so popular that they brought her back in the series version to play Beth's look-alike cousin! During this production she met her future husband, Rick Mansfield, who worked on the set as a lighting technician. They are now divorced.

The Bradys came knocking again, and Eve resurrected her role as Jan on "The Brady Brides" in 1981, "A Very Brady Christmas" in 1988, and the short-lived "Bradys" series in 1990. She (wisely) declined to do the abysmal *Brady Bunch Variety Hour* in 1976.

Eve also played the wife of "Mod Squad's" Clarence Williams III in the 1988 comedy film *I'm Gonna Git You Sucka*. In one scene, she sends her kids off to watch TV; you guessed it, they tune in just in time to catch "The Brady Bunch" theme song. It's a must-rent!

More recently, Eve has appeared as part of the ensemble cast of The Groundlings, a Los Angeles comedy team in the same vein as Saturday Night Live. In addition, she has done several plays.

✿   ✿   ✿

Spotlight on Eve Plumb

Favorite performer: Katharine Hepburn.

If I couldn't be an actor I would: "Do something with plants."

First job: Final Touch fabric softener commercial.

Worst job: "Some of the scary theatre I did."

Favorite Brady Bunch memory: "I took home Myron the mouse and when I went on vacation Mrs. Whitfield [the studio school teacher] took care of him and even took him to the vet when he got sick."

Favorite episode: "The Grand Canyon ones."

Do you mind being associated with "The Brady Bunch"? (to writer Max Merlin): "Imagine if you were known for something in high school, like some sporting event, and then when anybody saw you that's what they wanted to talk about. You'd get pretty sick of it after awhile. Even if it was a wonderful thing, and this was, and is. It's just like a twilight zone kind of thing, and you feel like everybody's answer to a Trivial Pursuit question. So it can be frustrating at times."

✿   ✿   ✿

Eve Plumb's Credits

AS A REGULAR	"The Brady Bunch," ABC, 1969-1974; "The Brady Kids," ABC, 1972-1974; "Little Women," NBC, 1979; "The Brady Brides," NBC, 1981; "A Very Brady Christmas," CBS, 1988; "The Bradys," CBS, 1990.
TV SERIES	"The Big Valley," ABC; "The Virginian," NBC, 1967; "Family Affair," CBS, 1968; "Lancer," CBS, 1968; "Mannix," CBS, 1968; "It Takes A Thief," ABC; "Lassie," CBS; "Gunsmoke," CBS, 1969; "Adam 12," NBC; "Here's Lucy," CBS, 1972; "Tales of the Unexpected," NBC, 1977; "Wonder Woman," CBS, 1977; "The Love Boat," ABC, 1980; "Fantasy Island," ABC, 1981; "The Facts of Life," NBC; "On The Television," Nickelodeon; "The Great Sitcom Search," Nickelodeon; "Murder, She Wrote," CBS; "Lois & Clark," ABC, 1994.

TV MOVIES, SPECIALS, PILOTS AND MINI-SERIES

"In Name Only," ABC, 1969; "The House on Greenapple Road," ABC, 1970; "The ABC Afterschool Special: Sara's Summer Of The Swans," (with Christopher Knight) ABC, 1974; "Dawn: Portrait of a Teenage Runaway," NBC, 1976; "Alexander: The Other Side of Dawn," NBC, 1977; "Telethon," ABC, 1977; "Little Women," NBC, 1978; "Secrets of Three Hungry Wives," NBC, 1978; "Greatest Heroes Of The Bible: The Story of Noah," NBC, 1978; "The Night the Bridge Fell Down," NBC, 1983; "A Very Brady Christmas," CBS, 1988.

MOVIES

I'm Gonna Get You Sucka, 1988; *And God Spoke*, 1994.

THEATRE

Slumber Party; *Frayed Knots* (Improv comedy); *Feminine Hijinks* (Stand up comedy duo); *Girls Club*; *Your Very Own TV Show*; *South Pacific*, Bucks County Playhouse, 1991; *The Real Live Brady Bunch*, Chicago, 1991—as Tami Cutler from episode #98, "Adios Johnny Bravo"; *Charles Manson, The Musical* (as Sharon Tate and Rosemary LaBianca; Eve credited herself as Betty Huron).

THE CAST, THEN AND NOW

SUSAN OLSEN

> "Pigtails was the hairdo I really liked. Then it became my job and I hated them. [On the show] they kept bleaching my hair, and it started to fall out. The hairdresser told Sherwood, and he said if worst came to worst we'd just cut my hair off and have fake curls like Buffy [the character on "Family Affair"]. At that point, I hit the roof!"

Susan Marie Olsen, the youngest of the Brady clan, is also the youngest of the Olsen clan. Born in Santa Monica, California, on August 14, 1961, to Lawrence and DeLoice ("Dee") Olsen, she made her TV debut in a fabric softener commercial when she was fourteen months old. (By a singular coincidence, Eve Plumb's first job in show business was also in a fabric softener commercial.)

Then.

While her father worked for Douglas Aircraft, her mother presided over the kids' showbiz careers. Larry Joe, the oldest and some twenty years Susan's senior, got his start in the feature *Happy Land* (1938, Don Ameche) and later appeared in *Who Killed Doc Robin?* (1948, Virginia Grey). Susan's brother, Christopher, also made his screen debut at fourteen months—in *Behind the Iron Curtain* (1948, Dana Andrews) as well as playing Doris Day's kidnapped son in Hitchcock's *The Man Who Knew Too Much* (1956). Her sister, Diane, only three years older, retired at a young age but almost came back to appear in "The Brady Bunch" episode "The Slumber Caper" [#30] along-

Now.

side a number of other Brady real-life relatives. But because of final exams at a rigorous private school, she bowed out.

While in kindergarten, Susan was chosen to sing "I'm A Believer" on Pat Boone's daytime show, and soon afterward she made her acting debut in January, 1968, on "Ironside." After appearing in episodes of "Gunsmoke" and "Julia," she landed the role of Cindy on "The Brady Bunch" three days after her seventh birthday.

When the series ended, Susan, like many other child stars, encountered the problem of being typecast; acting was put on the back burner. She graduated from William Howard Taft High School in Woodland Hills and went on to attend Pierce Community College and The American Academy of Dramatic Arts. In 1979, she did commercials advertising the "Sindy" doll for the Louis Marx Company.

While in school she met her future husband, Steve Ventimiglia, who was then a student in San Francisco. At his suggestion they formed Man In Space, a company specializing in product design. Together they developed a successful line of glow-in-the-dark, animal print sneakers, which they sold to Converse. The kids' line is called "Kids Glow," and the adult line, "Glow All Stars." Susan also illustrates books and designs textile prints.

She is currently divorced and lives in the Los Angeles area.

Spotlight On Susan Olsen

Favorite Performer: Elvis Presley.

The person I would most like to meet: Jimmy Page.

If I had more time I would: "Ride horses."

If I couldn't be an actor, I would be: "A musician."

First job: Downy Fabric Softener commercial.

Worst job: "The Brady Bunch Variety Hour."

Favorite Brady Bunch memory: "I was coming back for the new show ["The Bradys"], and it was my first day and I was scared and nervous. Florence and Bob were on the set; I had the same sense of calm that a nervous child would have in seeing her parents. And that was the moment I knew that this is family."

Favorite episode: "The one where Greg and Peter go on a double date ["Peter and the Wolf," #100]. That was the year the scripts almost got good."

Least favorite episode: "The Shirley Temple one ["The Snooperstar," #113]. That ranks up there with one of the most embarrassing moments of my life."

Most frequently asked questions: "Are you dead (confusion with Anissa Jones, Buffy on 'Family Affair')?" "Are you messed up?" "Why weren't you on 'A Very Brady Christmas?' " (She was on her honeymoon.)

How I most resemble Cindy: "Well, I look like her a lot!"

How I don't resemble Cindy: "I don't resemble Cindy in that she tattles on her friends. I was a tomboy and Cindy was a nice girl. She's the kind of girl . . . we would have egged her locker!"

Susan Olsen's Credits

| **AS A REGULAR** | "The Brady Bunch," ABC, 1969-1974; "The Brady Kids," ABC, 1972-1974; "The Brady Bunch Hour," ABC, 1977; "The Bradys, CBS," 1990. |

| **TV SERIES** | "Ironside," NBC, 1968; "Gunsmoke," CBS, 1968; |

"Gunsmoke," CBS, 1969; "Julia," NBC; "The Wonderful World of Disney: The Boy Who Stole The Elephants," NBC, 1970.

TV MOVIES, SPECIALS AND PILOTS   "The Brady Bunch Variety Hour," ABC, 1976; "The Brady Girls Get Married," NBC, 1981; "Bradymania!," ABC, 1993; "Salute To The 70s," NBC, 1993; "The MTV Movie Awards," MTV, 1993 (as Cindy Brady).

MOVIES   *The Trouble With Girls*, 1969 (with Elvis Presley and featuring Susan's prime-time clone, Anissa "Buffy" Jones); *The Brady Bunch*, 1995 (as a reporter for the *National Tattler*).

ROBBIE RIST

Born in California's San Fernando Valley on April 4, 1964, Robbie Rist was the only one of his family to enter into show business. His father is an electrical engineer, his mother is a floral designer, and his sister is a respiratory therapist/nurse.

An avid horror film buff, Robbie wanted more than anything to be in one and convinced his parents to take him to an agent. At the time he was seven years old and attending Winnetka Elementary School. Shortly thereafter he got his first job in a Nestle's Crunch commercial, and some two hundred commercials followed.

Then.

In 1974, in an attempt to bring back a younger audience to "The Brady Bunch," Robbie was cast as Cousin Oliver. He appeared in the last six episodes before the show was canceled.

Currently, Robbie heads a band called Wonderboy, acting as musician, singer, and songwriter. The group performs locally around the Los Angeles area.

Robbie has been to London twice to work on Steven Spielberg's forthcoming animated feature *Snowballs*. Robbie also continues his voice-over work in commercials for Pizza Hut, Bud Light, Kellogg's cereal, and a

Now.

number of others. He is one of the voices on Coca Cola's innovative talking ice cubes commercial, now getting a good deal of exposure in theatres in Europe.

Spotlight on Robbie Rist

Favorite performer: John Lithgow.

The person I would most like to meet: Elvis Costello.

If I had more time I would: "I would probably be bored out of my mind. I have an almost unnatural amount of free time."

First job: Nestle's Crunch commercial.

Worst job: "I never really had a bad job."

Brady Bunch memory: "I was on the teeter-totter with Susan [Olsen] between scenes and we had this fun little game where the person who was closer to the ground would bump the bottom end of the teeter-totter and the other would bump up a little bit. Well, Susan went down a little hard and I sailed over the front of the bars and landed on my face and slid down to her and split my mouth wide open. I cried—a lot."

Most frequently asked question: "You were that kid, weren't you?"

How I resemble Oliver: "We're both trapped in a world we never made."

Robbie Rist's Credits

| AS A REGULAR | "The Brady Bunch," ABC, 1974; "Lucas Tanner," NBC, 1974-1975; "The Mary Tyler Moore Show," CBS, 1976-1977; "The Bionic Woman," ABC/NBC, 1976-1978; "Big John, Little John," NBC, 1976-1977; "Galactica 1980," ABC, 1980; "Kidd Video," NBC, 1984-1987. |

| TV SERIES | "CHiPS," NBC; "Simon & Simon," CBS; "Knight Rider," NBC, 1985. |

| TV MOVIES, SPECIALS, AND PILOTS | "The ABC Afterschool Special: Alexander," ABC, 1973; "The John Denver Show—A Family Event," ABC, 1974; "The Paul Lynde Comedy Hour," ABC, 1975; "The Ted Knight Musical Comedy Variety Special," CBS, 1976; "The ABC Short Story Special: My Dear Uncle Sherlock," ABC, 1977; "Instant Family," NBC, 1977; "Having Babies II," ABC, 1977; "Little Lulu," ABC, 1978; "Gossip," NBC, 1979; "Solitary Man," CBS, 1979; "Aunt Mary," CBS, 1979; "The Great American Traffic Jam," NBC, 1980; "Through The Magic Pyramid," NBC, 1981. |

| MOVIES | *Memory Of Us*, 1974; *He Is My Brother*, 1976; *Iron Eagle*, 1986; *Dirty Laundry*, 1987; *Teenage Mutant Ninja Turtles*, 1990, as the voice of Michelangelo; *Teenage Mutant Ninja Turtles II: The Secret Of The Ooze*, 1991, as the voice of Michelangelo; *Teenage Mutant Ninja Turtles III: Back in Time*, 1993 as the voice of Michelangelo; *Snowballs*, 1994 (voice over). |

ANN B. DAVIS

(To the author, when asked about production spe-
cifics): "It's just hard to remember what the me-
chanics were. We were shooting a pilot—we didn't
know we were starting a cult!"

Then.

Now.

Ann Bradford Davis and her identical twin
sister, Harriet, were born to Cassius and Margue-
rite Davis on May 5, 1926 in Schenectady, New
York. When Ann was three the family moved to
Erie, Pennsylvania, where her father worked as
an electrical engineer for the Erie Works. Ann and
her older brother, Evans, must have inherited
their acting genes from their mother, who performed in local theatre groups.

But Ann didn't always want to be in show
business. Originally she enrolled as a pre-med
major at the University of Michigan, while her
sister, also there, chose drama. It wasn't until
she went to see her brother's performance in
Oklahoma! that she changed her mind. Ann
graduated in 1948 with a degree in drama and
speech. John Rich, who directed the first six
episodes of "The Brady Bunch," was one of
her classmates.

An actor's life wasn't easy, and Ann took
work wherever she could get it. Upon graduation she stayed in Erie and performed at the
Erie Playhouse, then relocated to the West
Coast. There she did the rounds, performing in
local theatre groups, comedy clubs, and coffee
houses. To make ends meet she worked in a department store.

In 1955 Ann got her big break. A friend's
boyfriend, who was a casting director, saw her act and suggested that she

audition for "The Bob Cummings Show." Ann won the part and played Charmaine "Shultzy" Schultz for five successful years and earned four Emmy nominations; she won twice. On February 9, 1960, Ann received a star on the Hollywood Walk Of Fame!

During hiatuses Ann continued to perform in regional theater, as well as touring Vietnam, Korea, and Thailand with the USO, an organization she strongly supports to this day.

In 1969 Ann landed the role of Alice in "The Brady Bunch." She would return for all its spinoff incarnations. In 1976, she sold her house in Los Angeles to move to Denver, Colorado, where she joined an Episcopal community led by Bishop William C. Frey. Recently the community relocated to Ambridge, Pennsylvania.

Ann continues her theatre work and can be seen occasionally on TV.

✿   ✿   ✿

Spotlight On Ann B. Davis

Favorite performers: Bea Lillie and Eve Arden.

I always wanted to meet: "I met everyone I wanted to meet. I get around!"

First job: "I was paid $2 for a puppet show I did with my sister back when I was a Girl Scout."

Worst job: "No job is a worst job. If you're working, you're working."

Favorite episode: "The one in which I get dunked [#57, "My Sister, Benedict Arnold"]. It was 120 degrees on the set that day and I worked all day hoping to get to that part where I got socked with some nice cold water."

How I resemble Alice: "Alice was an extension of myself. When you're doing a television thing, you don't have too much time for character analysis. So in your own mind you build a character that is as much like yourself as you can."

Most frequently asked question: "Do you keep in touch?" (Yes.)

Ann B. Davis' Credits

AS A REGULAR	"The Bob Cummings Show," NBC, 1955/CBS, 1955-57/NBC, 1957-59; "The Keefe Brasselle Show," CBS, 1963; "The John Forsythe Show," NBC, 1965-66; "The Brady Bunch," ABC, 1969-1974; "The Brady Bunch Hour," ABC, 1977; "The Brady Brides," NBC, 1981; "The Bradys," CBS, 1990.
TV SERIES	"Eddie Cantor Comedy Theatre," syndicated; "Art Linkletter's House Party," CBS, 1957; "The Perry Como Show," NBC, 1958; "Arthur Murray Party," NBC, 1959; "Wagon Train," NBC, 1960; "McKeever and the Colonel," NBC, 1963; "The Bob Hope Chrysler Theatre," NBC, 1964; "The Dating Game," ABC, 1969; "Love American Style," ABC, 1971; "The Love Boat," ABC, 1980; "Day By Day," NBC, 1989 (as Alice); "The People Next Door," CBS, 1989; "Butterfly Island," Christian Broadcasting Network, 1990; "Hi Honey, I'm Home," Nickelodeon, 1991.
TV MOVIES, SPECIALS AND PILOTS	"R.B. and Myrnalene," 1962, pilot; "The Brady Bunch Variety Hour," ABC, 1976; "A Very Brady Christmas," CBS, 1988.

| MOVIES | *A Man Called Peter*, 1955; *Pepe*, 1960; *All Hands On Deck*, 1961; *Lover Come Back*, 1961; *Naked Gun 33⅓*, 1994 (as Alice); *The Brady Bunch*, 1995 (as a truck driver). |

MOVIES | *A Man Called Peter*, 1955; *Pepe*, 1960; *All Hands On Deck*, 1961; *Lover Come Back*, 1961; *Naked Gun 33⅓*, 1994 (as Alice); *The Brady Bunch*, 1995 (as a truck driver).

THEATRE | *Auntie Mame*; *Blithe Spirit*; *Funny Girl*; *Once Upon a Mattress*, Broadway, 1960; *The Nearlyweds*, 1988 (written by Lloyd Schwartz); *Rockers*, 1993 (written by Sherwood Schwartz); *Crazy For You*, 1994.

EMMY AWARDS AND NOMINATIONS | "The Bob Cummings Show," supporting actress nomination, 1955; "The Bob Cummings Show," supporting actress nomination, 1956; "The Bob Cummings Show," supporting actress in a drama or comedy series, award, 1957; "The Bob Cummings Show," supporting actress in a drama or comedy series, award, 1958-59.

ALLAN MELVIN

"Six feet tall, two hundred pounds of unbudgeable bachelor."

The son of a film salesman, Allan Melvin was born on February 18, 1923, in Kansas City, Missouri, but grew up in the Bronx. He recalls becoming interested in show business through the influence of his father, and an aunt and uncle who performed in vaudeville.

Allan graduated from Evander Childs High School in the Bronx and took extension courses in journalism at Columbia University. While he worked as an usher at the Crest Theatre, he practiced imitating voices and doing impressions. In 1946 he won an Arthur Godfrey Talent Show, which led to work in radio on such shows as "Lorenzo Jones" and "Pepper Young's Family."

Allan made the rounds doing stand-up comedy written for him by novelist Richard Condon. In 1951, when Condon's book *Stalag 17* was produced for the Broadway stage, Allan played the role of Reed for two years.

He made his television debut in 1954 playing an airline pilot on "Valiant Lady," a CBS daytime soap opera. In 1955 he went on to play Corporal Henshaw on "The Phil Silvers Show." In 1961 Allan relocated to California and more television work followed, including "The Andy Griffith Show," "Gomer Pyle," "The Dick Van Dyke Show," and "My Favorite Martian."

His part as Sam the butcher came in 1969, but he chose not to reprise the role in any of the subsequent Brady spin-offs. Following "The Brady Bunch," Allan won the role as next-door neighbor Barney Hefner on "All In The Family," which he played for five years. He continued this role on "Archie Bunker's Place" for another three years.

Allan also did voice work for over twenty-five cartoon series, including such cartoon characters as Bluto on "Popeye" and Magilla on "Magilla Gorilla." He also played the Liquid Plummr man.

Allan lives in the Los Angeles area and enjoys golf, sailing, and reading.

❀   ❀   ❀

Allan Melvin's Credits

| AS A REGULAR | "Lorenzo Jones," radio; "Pepper Young's Family," radio; "Valiant Lady," CBS, 1954-55; "The Phil Silvers Show," CBS, 1955-59; "The Dick Van Dyke Show," CBS, 1961-66; "The Magilla Gorilla Show," syndicated, 1964; "Gomer Pyle, USMC," CBS, 1965-69; "The Banana Splits Adventure Hour," NBC, 1968-70; "The Brady Bunch," ABC, 1969-74; "Yogi's Gang," ABC, 1973-75; "All In The Family," CBS, 1973-79; "Partridge Family: 2200 A.D.," CBS, 1974-75; "The All New Popeye Hour," CBS, 1978-81; "Archie Bunker's Place," CBS, 1979-83.

TV SERIES | "Route 66," CBS, 1961; "The Andy Griffith Show," CBS, 1962-64, 4 appearances; "Empire," NBC, 1963; "McHale's Navy," ABC, 1963; "Grindl," NBC, 1963; "The Danny Thomas Show," CBS, 1964; "The Joey Bishop Show," CBS, 1965, 4 appearances; "My Favorite Martian," CBS, 1964 and 1966, 2 appearances; "Ben Casey," ABC, 1964; "Slattery's People," CBS, 1965; "Run, Buddy, Run," CBS, 1966; "Love American Style," ABC, 1969-71, 3 appearances; "All in the Family," CBS, 1971.

TV SPECIALS AND PILOTS | "Barnaby," 1965; "Alfred of the Amazon," CBS, 1967; "We'll Take Manhattan," CBS, 1968; "Man in the Middle," CBS, 1972; "The Tiny Tree," NBC, 1975.

MOVIES | *With Six You Get Eggroll*, 1968.

THEATRE | *Stalag 17*, 48th Street Theatre, New York, 1951.

TIGER

Why was this dog quietly written out of the show?

It would take a highly trained eye to detect that four different dogs were used to play Tiger: Chip, Ruckus, Tiger 1, and Tiger 2.

Sherwood Schwartz initially hired veteran animal trainer Frank Inn to do the pilot. Inn, who owned and trained Chip and Ruckus, was also responsible for the talents of Tramp, Arnold the Pig, and Benji. In fact, Inn and fellow trainer Judd Weatherwax (Lassie) are the only two animal trainers to be inducted into the Academy of Motion Picture Arts and Sciences Hall of Fame. You couldn't get any better.

But for a reason no one remembers, Lou Schumacher's company was hired to do the series, and they brought in a look-alike dog, Tiger 1, who shortly thereafter bit the big one. Exactly how is unclear. Says Schumacher, "He jumped out of the truck and got hit by a car." Karl Miller, Schumacher's head trainer disagrees. "I seem to remember he chewed his way out of a screen cage in back of the truck and ran away." You decide who to believe!

In any case, another look-alike dog was found at the pound. With the help of a little Frost and Tip, and a snip here and there—voilà, Tiger 2. Who could tell? An inexperienced, Tiger 2 got on-the-job training, making his debut on the episode where Jan is allergic to his flea powder (#4, "Katchoo"). Because of his initial unpredictability, Sherwood wrote him out of the script, but later realized the dog had made great progress. After all, can *your* dog jump on top of his doghouse?

Tiger 2 worked on other shows concurrently with "The Brady Bunch." He appeared as an atmosphere dog on "Kung Fu," the series (ABC, 1973), and in the feature *Winged Colt* (1977). In 1976 Tiger 2 won a PATSY (Performing Animal Top Stars of the Year) award for his work on the film A Boy and His Dog, starring Don Johnson. He even beat out Jack the dog from "Little House on the Prairie." In 1977, Tiger, now an old dog of eleven, was supposed to appear in Peter Yates's *The Deep*, but his trainer was fired. Tiger 2 died of old age in 1979.

FLUFFY

Actually, there were thirty-six "Rhubarb" cats who may have played Fluffy. Exactly which did is unknown.

The "Rhubarb" cats, owned and trained by Frank Inn, got their name from a cat in H. Allen Smith's 1951 film adaptation about a cat who inherits Brooklyn's baseball team. Although many cats were used interchangeably, "Rhubarb" was presented to the public as one cat.

One or more of these cats played Fluffy.
Take your pick.

THE REAL HEAD OF THE BRADY FAMILY— SHERWOOD SCHWARTZ

Sherwood Charles Schwartz, the creator of "The Brady Bunch," was born on November 14, 1916, in Passaic, New Jersey, the middle child of Herman, a whole- sale grocer, and Rose Schwartz. The family moved to the Bronx when Sherwood was twelve. Graduating from DeWitt Clinton High School, Sher- wood entered New York University to pursue a career in medicine. He received his Masters in biologi- cal sciences and psy- chology at the

Sherwood Schwartz today, with a gift from Ann B. Davis.

University of Southern California in Los Angeles.

But his goal of becoming a doctor never came to fruition. Instead, he wound up writing jokes alongside his older brother Al on "The Bob Hope Radio Show."

Since radio was a thirty nine-week business, Sherwood spent his thirteen-week hiatus on the East Coast. On the boardwalk in Far Rockaway, New Jersey, he met his wife, Mildred. About one-and-a-half years later, on December 6, 1941, he proposed via telegram. The next day the U.S. entered World War II. The couple were married on December 22, 1941, and Sherwood entered the Army as a corporal. During his service he polished his craft writing for the Armed Forces Radio Service. One of his sergeants, George Rosenberg, would become his agent and entree into television.

Sherwood landed his first TV writing job on "I Married Joan" (NBC, 1952-1955), followed by a seven-year stint on "The Red Skelton Show." Eventually he became the show's head writer and won an Emmy in 1960 with his brother Al and the other staff writers. His other brother, Elroy, was also a comedy writer, and later all three brothers would write for "The Brady Bunch."

In 1963 Sherwood tried on a producer's hat and gave birth to his first cult classic, "Gilligan's Island" (CBS, 1964-1967). "The Brady Bunch" followed in 1969.

Sherwood's other credits include "It's About Time" (CBS, 1966-1967), about two astronauts who land in a prehistoric world and befriend a stoneage family; "Dusty's Trail" (1973, syndicated, Bob Denver), about a Conestoga wagon separated from the rest of the train somewhere in the Old West; "Big John, Little John" (NBC, 1976-1977), a Saturday-morning show starring Herb Edelman and Robbie "Cousin Oliver" Rist; and the first half-season of "Harper Valley, P.T.A.," starring Barbara Eden (NBC, 1981-1982). Sherwood also collaborated with Michael Jacobs on the short-lived "Together We Stand" (CBS, 1986). Much like "The Brady Bunch" episode "Kelly's Kids" [#107], it involved a couple and their newly adopted multiracial kids.

On December 22, 1991, Sherwood and Mildred Schwartz celebrated their fiftieth wedding anniversary. Together they have produced a bunch of their own: Don (an ophthamologist), Lloyd (Sherwood's writing/producing partner), Ross (an entertainment lawyer) and Hope (a writer and creator of "The Housewives").

Sherwood is busy working on two "Gilligan's Island" projects. One is a theatrical musical and the other a feature film. Both will have an all-new set of castaways.

❁   ❁   ❁

Selected Videography

WRITING CREDITS
"I Married Joan," NBC, 1952-54; "The Red Skelton Show," CBS, 1954-62; "My Favorite Martian," CBS, 1963.

SERIES— CREATOR/ WRITER/ PRODUCER
"Gilligan's Island," CBS, 1964-74; "It's About Time," CBS, 1966-67; "The Brady Bunch," ABC, 1969-74; "The Brady Kids," ABC, 1972-74; "Dusty's Trail," syndicated, 1973-74; "The New Adventures of Gilligan," ABC, 1974-76; "Big John, Little John," NBC, 1976-77; "Harper Valley P.T.A.," NBC, 1981-82; "The Brady Brides," NBC, 1981; "Gilligan's Planet," ABC, 1982-83; "Together We Stand," CBS, 1986; "The Bradys," CBS, 1990.

MOVIES MADE FOR TELEVISION
"Rescue from Gilligan's Island," NBC, 1978; "The Castaways on Gilligan's Island," NBC, 1979; "The Harlem Globetrotters on Gilligan's Island," NBC, 1981; "The Invisible Woman," NBC, 1983; "A Very Brady Christmas," CBS, 1988.

THEATRE
Gilligan's Island: The Musical, premiered at The Flatrock Playhouse, North Carolina; also played in Chicago and San Diego, 1993; *Rockers*, premiered at The Flatrock Playhouse, North Carolina, 1993. (Both pieces were written by Sherwood Schwartz.)

4222 CLINTON WAY—THE HAPPIEST PLACE ON EARTH!

Susan Olsen (explaining why Tiger's doghouse remained in the backyard despite his disappearance:) "One of the studio lights fell down and crashed in the backyard and burned a hole in the astroturf, and they put the doghouse on top to hide it!"

The real thing, sans fake window.

Face it, this is TV-land, and in TV-land, there *is* no reality. So if you imagined for a minute that the Brady house is a real house, you can put that idea right out of your head. Granted, the *exterior* is that of a real house, one located in Studio City, California. In order to make it appear to be a two-story house, a fake window was hung from the roof. (Why the network couldn't find a bonafide two-story house, preferably one with an attic, remains a mystery.)

The interiors, of course, were sets, created by set designers on Stage 5 of Paramount Studios. In case you wondered, the sets used in "A Very Brady Christmas" and "The Bradys" were not the originals—but were, to the exact inch, the same *as* the originals. According to Sherwood, requests for blueprints of the Brady house are on his Most Frequently Asked Questions List—right up there with "Do the coconuts that hit Gilligan really hurt?" Here are some more vexing questions about the Brady domicile—and their answers.

1. How is it that the girls' room, the boys' room, and Greg's attic room *all* overlook the backyard? Answer: Because the stories required it. We, as viewers, aren't supposed to remember, or question, the interior layout.

2. Did Alice have a bathroom? Answer: She probably did, but she definitely did *not* have a toilet; none of the Bradys had toilets. They were taken out by the Broadcast Standards Department. However, Mike and Carol *were* allowed to sleep in the same bed, a milestone in television history. (Only a few years earlier, Rob and Laura Petrie were denied this pleasure.) By the way, a new bathroom was added to the right of the main staircase for *A Very Brady Christmas*.

3. Where did that big attic in which the boys camp out in episode #77, "Fright Night," come from? Answer: No rational explanation here. In the episode where Greg wants his own room and ends up getting the den, Mike firmly states that "the attic is $2\frac{1}{2}$ feet tall!" (#43, "Our Son, The Man.")

4. Why were there two completely different service porches at different times? Answer: Maybe because Mike is an architect and

he remodeled. And while we're on the subject of entrances, where did the new service porch and two backyard entrances *lead* to?

5. Where did the Bradys keep the tepee, trampoline, ski slope, clubhouse, ping-pong table, dunking booth, soap box car, and the S.S. Brady boat? Answer: Possibly in the Mystery Room at the top of the main staircase. Have a better idea?

There are countless other strange inconsistencies within the show, ranging from the mobile barbecue to temporary walls to the bewildering array of cars Mike owned. The family station wagon always *appeared* to be the same, but in fact the Bradys had three different wagons (License plates 746 AEH, JOP 745, and Y18078). As for the red *and* blue convertibles, maybe they were company cars leased from Chrysler. Or Mike was loaded. Or something.

For the record, the Bradys had two phone numbers: 762-0799 (#38, "The Not-So-Ugly Duckling") and 555-6161 (#96, "Mail Order Hero"). Their official, if ambiguous, address was 4222 Clinton Way, City (#23, "Lost Locket, Found Locket").

The Brady House (downstairs)

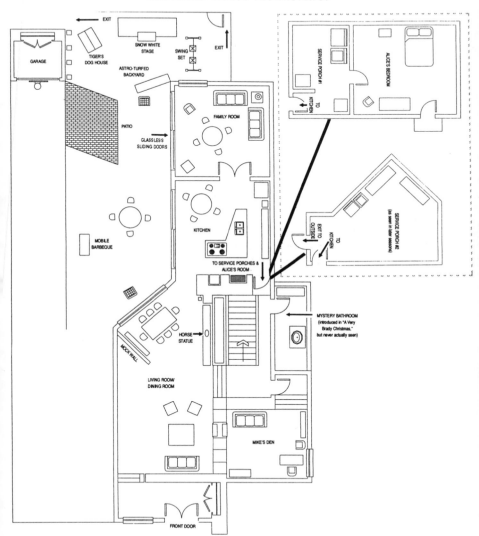

NOTE: All drawings are a composite and represent those floor plans most used in "The Brady Bunch."

FLOOR PLANS COURTESY: Robert Greenhood

The Brady House (upstairs)

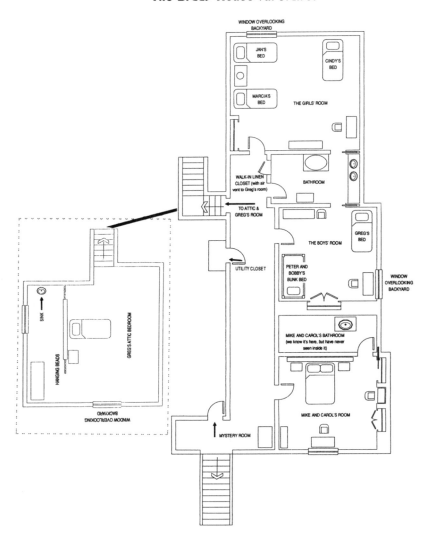

NOTE: All drawings are a composite and represent those floor plans most used in "The Brady Bunch."

FLOOR PLANS COURTESY: Robert Greenhood

DID YOU EVER WONDER . . . ?

Here are some things we never learned about the Bradys. Did you ever ask yourself . . .

What city the Bradys lived in?

What happened to Carol's first husband?

Why, if Mike designed the house for his big family, he didn't design more bedrooms for the kids?

What the name of Mike's company was?

Whether Alice ever got a day off, and, if so, who cooked when she did?

What happened to Tiger?

What happened to Fluffy?

What exactly happened when Raquel the goat spent the night in Greg's room?

PART TWO

THE WAY THEY ALL BECAME THE BRADY BUNCH

Everything You Always Wanted to Know and Then Some

IN THE BEGINNING . . .

The birth of "The Brady Bunch" (an interview with Sherwood Schwartz)

"Here's the story, of a lovely lady, who was bringing up three very lovely girls . . ." If there's one thing Sherwood Schwartz is famous for, it's the theme song lyrics he wrote for "Gilligan's Island" and "The Brady Bunch," the two shows he created and turned into TV legends. In fact, in his book *Inside Gilligan's Island* (an entertaining and joyful account), Sherwood describes a 1963 meeting with Jim Aubrey, then CBS's president of programming. Aubrey complained, "How the hell is the audience going to know what they're doing on the same damn island every week?" Sherwood replied, "There's a theme song that will take care of the problem. In sixty entertaining seconds, the lyrics will tell it all." (The music for "The Brady Bunch," by the way, was composed by Frank DeVol, who also composed the music for the themes of "My Three Sons" and "Family Affair").

If television has one cardinal sin, Sherwood explains, it's exposition. "TV is shorthand. The more you can assume from what you see immediately, the less explanation is required." "The Brady Bunch" was no exception. "A lot of dark-haired parents have blonde children and a lot of blonde parents have dark-haired children. But it's easier for the audience to understand if you have a blonde woman, three blonde children, and you say 'that's from that marriage,' and if you have a dark-haired man and three dark-haired boys, and you say, 'that's from that marriage.'" Why waste precious time explaining background, considering that a standard thirty minute program is broken down into roughly twenty minutes of actual show, with the rest commercials?

The initial idea for "The Brady Bunch" was something of a mixed marriage itself, coming as it did from the union of two different factors. Remembers Sherwood, "I read in the paper in 1966 that over 20 percent of all the marriages included a child from a previous marriage. I mean, that's one out of five marriages. That's a lot of people getting married who had previously been married. So that stuck in my head. That same week my daughter [Hope] came home from junior high school and told me about a boy in the class who was in a play and was very upset. His mother had remarried and he didn't know whether to give the ticket [only one was allotted per child] to his new father . . . or to his own mother. Now it's almost an amusing problem to adults, but to a child that's a very big decision. So coupling that with the statistic that I read, it seemed to me that this opened up a whole new field to situation family comedy that had never been done before." (This incident was used as the premise of "Eenie, Meenie, Mommy, Daddy," episode #5.)

But despite Sherwood's record of success with "Gilligan's Island," it took three years for "The Brady Bunch," originally titled "Yours And Mine," to get on the air. All three networks liked it, yet they all wanted to change it. If Sherwood had learned anything from his "Gilligan's Island" experience, it was to stick to his guns.

In *Inside Gilligan's Island*, Sherwood recalls the story of friend Phil Sharpe, writer/producer of "The Cara Williams Show": "He fought the same interminable battles with the networks for awhile that I was going through on 'Gilligan's Island'—battles of concept and characterizations. Finally, he succumbed to the pressure. He took what was the easy way out. He acceded to one demand after another from the network executives, and also from his star. He made all the changes they required. It was the only way, he felt, to preserve his sanity and still get on the air." The show was unsuccessful. "When a show is canceled," Sherwood notes, "it's not the network's fault, or the star's fault . . . it's the producer's fault. He's the one who caused the show to sink."

"The Brady Bunch" serves as a classic example of network interference endangering a great idea. ABC had just developed its ninety-minute "TV Movie Of The Week" idea and suggested that Sherwood expand his thirty-minute show (the pilot, entitled "The Honeymoon") to ninety minutes. Sherwood protested that he would have to "invent" the first sixty minutes. The material he had on hand could only cover the last third. ABC argued that they didn't want any additions. They just wanted him to prolong it. Sherwood replied, "I can't make it longer. I can't take a thirty-minute script and stretch it to ninety minutes. It will be pretty damn dull!"

Meanwhile, NBC was also interested, but they found the ending totally unbelievable. They felt that no couple on their honeymoon would *ever* go back to get their kids as the script required them to. If Mike and Carol Brady were called and told that one of the kids was sick, *then* they could return home. And *maybe* they would end up taking the whole bunch along. Sherwood pleaded that these people couldn't be completely happy without their children. NBC said the ending had to be changed. Sherwood said he couldn't change it.

CBS, for its part, wanted to make the pilot the sixth or seventh episode, intending to build up to the wedding. Creative control was clearly at issue. "The only reason I sold it [at all] is because a movie called *Yours, Mine and Ours* (Lucille Ball, Henry Fonda, 1968) came out and made a ton of money. ABC said, 'Hey, you know that show you were trying to sell us, well we'll do it your way.' So in effect that movie was my pilot." Ironically, the producers of that movie sued Sherwood for stealing their idea of joining two families. "I should have sued *them*," exclaimed Sherwood. In fact, his idea was registered with the Writers Guild long before the inception of the movie.

Nevertheless, to minimize confusion, Sherwood's "Yours and Mine" title had to be changed. Says Sherwood, "Networks test titles. They go to supermarkets and malls and ask, 'Would you watch a show called "The Brady Bunch"?' And the response they got was, 'No, we don't want to see a western.' The word 'bunch' was like *The Wild Bunch* [Ernest Borgnine, William Holden, 1969]; it was Jesse James and gangs. The word had outlaw kind of memories. Now, of course, 'bunch' is sweet, you think of 'Brady Bunch'! So then we tested 'Brady Brood' and people didn't like that. They thought of witches. Finally a wonderful thing happens—a deadline! You have to make a decision and go on the air, and I liked 'Brady Bunch.' " Sherwood Schwartz, a resolute and successful producer, got his way.

Unlike the case of the name "Gilligan," for which Sherwood spent weeks combing through phone books in search of just the right name, Sherwood can't recall where he found the name "Brady." Perhaps it was because he preferred hard letters like "b" and "g." As he recalls it, "I also like alliteration wherever possible . . . you remember 'Brady Bunch'— you bite it off. It's kind of a memorable phrase, it seemed to me." (Also under consideration were the names "Barton" and "Bradley," the later a name already "taken," by the Bradley family on CBS's "Petticoat Junction.") As for the other Brady names, Mike, Carol, Greg, and so on, there is no significance. No family names, no past loves, no previous marriages. In fact, Sherwood makes it a rule never to use names from his own family. (Incidentally, here's a bit of trivia for all of you "Gilligan's Island" buffs. Did you know that "Gilligan" was the title character's *last* name? "Willie" was his first name, but it was never used on the air, only in the written presentation.)

CASTING THE BUNCH

But "The Brady Bunch's" popularity did involve other people. Casting was an enormous undertaking, and Sherwood decided to tackle the selection of the six kids first, before the adult principals. From a field of 464 boys and girls ("and that's the number *I* saw," remarks Sherwood), twelve were chosen—three blonde girls, three brown haired girls, three blonde boys, and three brown haired boys. "Just one kid had only one meeting and I knew it was the answer immediately, and that was Susan Olsen (Cindy Brady). She had just shy of seven and it was one of the most incredible interviews I ever had. She just took over. Mike Lookinland (Bobby Brady), who was clearly the best little actor, had the wrong hair color and we had to dye it brown." As for the others, temperaments, physical similarities, and some experience were keynotes.

Remembers Barry Williams (Greg Brady): "In the year preceding 'The Brady Bunch' I was a guest star on two shows, 'Gomer Pyle' and 'That Girl.' John Rich directed both of them, and he was also in partnership with Sherwood on 'Gilligan's Island' and 'The Brady Bunch.' So there were a couple of those cattlecall scenes, three call-backs, and then I did a screen test. I was thrown a basketball and I came bouncing in and held the camera. The execs were there and some of the network people, I believe. John [Rich] was standing off camera and started asking me questions. That was the last I heard until a script arrived on my doorstep— September 29, 1968, and I know that because it was a Sunday, and on Monday [Barry's birthday] we began the first day of production on the pilot. Later I asked John if my being on those other shows had anything to do with my getting the part and he said, 'Well, you got the job didn't you?' That's the way he answered everything. So, I think as much as that may have helped, Paramount got the feeling that yes, I had some experi-

ence, I had worked with John success-
fully, and I was the right age, coloring,
and height."

As for the adult principals, Joyce
Bulifant (best known as Murray Slaugh-
ter's wife Marie on "The Mary Tyler
Moore Show") was originally set to play
Carol Brady. Recalls Sherwood, "Joyce
was very funny; she had a funny voice."
But the following week Florence Henderson came in and tested for the role.
Paramount liked the idea of Henderson
because of her critical acclaim as a stage
actress. Florence recalls, "I was out here
doing 'The Dean Martin Show' and my
agent called and said they're looking for
someone for the show. And I said that I

Joyce Bulifant was almost cast as Carol . . .

didn't want to live out here [in California; at the time she was living in
New York], I can't do a series. And he said to just go down and meet
them, and I did, and I was asked to stay and do a screen test. Well, I was

on my way to Houston to do my nightclub act, and I said, 'If you can get me
on a plane tonight, I'll stay.' So I went
home, learned the scene, came back, and
did the screen test. I got made up in the
makeup room of the 'Star Trek' set. William Shatner was there, I'll never forget
it! Then I flew back to Houston. The
next day I got a call to come back and
do the pilot, but I had to get out of the
[nightclub] engagement. So I got someone to fill in and promised them that if
the series was a hit, I would come back
and work for the same money, which I
did. And that was it!"

And Alice? "I became concerned
about the lady that had already been

. . . and Monty Margetts was almost cast
as Alice.

chosen to be the housekeeper [Alice], and that person was Monty Margetts," remembers Sherwood. "She was not a funny person, but that was against Joyce Bulifant. But now that I had Florence it seemed to me that I needed more comedy in the kitchen. I heard Ann B. Davis was available. She was an old love of mine from other series [most notably as Shultzy on "The Bob Cummings Show"]. A terrific comedienne, she had a natural comedy persona." Says Ann B., "At the time I was doing some nightclub work in Seattle which had developed out of my USO show that I had done in Vietnam and Korea. My agent called and said Sherwood wanted to meet me. So they flew me down in the morning, drove me quickly out to the valley where he lived, and I met with him for all of half an hour. Then they rushed me back to the airport, threw me on the plane so I could do the show that evening. I found out a couple of days later that he did indeed want to use me, so they had to buy my way out of my nightclub act to come down and shoot the pilot."

As for casting the patriarch, Mike Brady, Gene Hackman was Sherwood's first choice, but "he had never done a television series . . . It was the year before he made *The French Connection*, so he was an unknown [actor], and Paramount said no."

Jeffrey Hunter, most recognizable for his role as Jesus Christ in the 1961 movie *King of Kings*, as well as for playing "Star Trek's" Captain Christopher Pike in the original series pilot, desperately wanted to play Mike Brady. "He was too handsome," Sherwood recalls. "I said to him, 'The guy on this show is an architect, not a model or an actor.' And he said, 'Look at my face! I'm getting wrinkles around my eyes! I'm getting lines in my face!'" As it happened, Hunter died in 1969 at the age of 43 during what would have been the first season of the show.

Gene Hackman as Mike Brady? It could have happened.

Ultimately cast as Mike Brady was Robert Reed, best known for his role opposite E.G. Marshall on "The Defenders" (1961-1965). Under contract with Paramount at the time, he tested for three different pilots: for the series version of the hit Broadway play *Barefoot In the Park*, which he had just done in New York, as well as for the series version of *Houseboat* [Cary Grant, Sophia Loren, 1958] and "The Brady Bunch." Remembers Ann B., "Bob wanted to do either of the other two, but not 'The Brady Bunch.' He wanted to be a *dramatic* actor." Robert Reed assessed his situation in the April, 1970, issue of *TV Guide*, saying, "I thought the show was going to be something else—that it was going to be more realistic. The pilot turned out to be 'Gilligan's Island' with kids—full of gags and gimmicks. At first I went along and decided to do the best I could . . . Now I argue on the set, and I think the show is better."

Jeffrey Hunter, who played Jesus Christ and the first starship captain on *Star Trek*, wanted to play Mike Brady—but lost out to Robert Reed.

Reed's misgivings about the show would lead to later conflicts. "We had many altercations," remembers Sherwood. "We were doing a scene in the kitchen where Florence and Ann B. were each making strawberry preserves [#80, "Jan, The Only Child"]. So, I'm in my office and I get a call to come down to the stage because Bob had walked out. He's in his dressing room, and naturally, it's up to me to find out what the problem is. The scene is lit, everybody's ready, and he just walked out without saying a word. So I asked him what the problem was and he said, 'If you don't know what the problem is, I can't explain it.' And I said, 'Well, let's try English.' He asked if I read the script, which is a direct insult because not only have I read the script, my rewrite is always the last script that goes to xerox for distribution! I said yes, and he said, 'You still don't know what I'm talking about?' And I said, 'no.' 'Are you familiar with the scene we're doing on stage?' he asked. Now, that's an insult to me as the producer because obviously I should know what they're doing. Then he said, 'I'm supposed to come into the kitchen and look in, and see them cooking these strawberries and I'm supposed to say, "Hey, this smells like strawberry heaven." ' And I said, 'Well, I just didn't want you to say, "Hi honey, I'm home." It's no joke or anything, it's just another way of saying "I'm here."' He said, 'You really don't know, do you?' And I said, 'No, I don't know. Tell me.' And he said, 'It just so happens that strawberries, while they're cooking, have no odor. So how can I take a breath and say it smells like strawberry heaven?' I said, 'Bob, I walked here, across the stage. You can smell strawberries in the kitchen, in the living room, in the bedroom area; you can smell strawberries all over the set!' Now he said to me, 'Do you want me to believe you or the *Encyclopedia Britannica*?' I said, 'Go out and smell it,' and he wouldn't, so I said, 'Okay, suppose you come in, look in the archway and say that it *looks* like strawberry heaven.' 'Oh,' he said, 'I can do that.'" (Actually, the line he ended up saying was, "Hi honey, I'm home. Hey, I do believe I've died and gone to strawberry heaven!")

Remarked Sherwood in the April 1970 issue of *TV Guide*, "This isn't a hokey series, but Bob is so used to 'Defenders' reality that he can't get used to situation comedy reality . . . He's always on the phone to the Los Angeles *Times* or the Police Department, or looking in the encyclopedia to check some matter of fact. His attitude is one of pure logic . . . But these qualities of sincerity and honesty come across on the screen and contribute to the character. That's why I think Bob does such a good job in the role. But if I—a situation comedy producer—were hired by 'The Defenders,' I wouldn't try to tell them how to run the show!"

Florence remembers, "Bob was always questioning whether something would work. We were doing the episode where I was supposed to take over his job and he mine [#8, "The Grass Is Always Greener"]. Anyway, it was a very funny scene where Bob was supposed to be getting stuff out of the refrigerator. He was supposed to drop an egg and slip on it, and he said that it was total nonsense, it will never work. And I said that before you shoot something down, try it. And, of course, in getting all the stuff out, he actually dropped an egg and took such a fall!" "I can add to that story," recalls Ann B., "because he was making rather a fuss! I swear, he hit the ground before the egg did! And, once I found out if he was all right, that he didn't hurt himself, I said, 'Do you think you can play it now?' And he looked up and said, 'You know, all the way down I was thinking that I deserved this!'

Temperamental leading men, mismatching hair colors, last-minute changes, and other assorted crises aside, that's the way they all became "The Brady Bunch."

BRADY MECHANICS: THE PRODUCTION

"The Brady Bunch" was filmed at Paramount Studios on Stage 5, keeping good company with hit TV productions like "Mission Impossible," "Love American Style," and "The Odd Couple." To direct the first six episodes of the show, Sherwood hired show biz veteran John Rich, who had also played a significant role in the creation and ultimate success of "Gilligan's Island." Having witnessed his versatility with shows from "The Dick Van Dyke Show" to "Bonanza," Sherwood was confident Rich would set the pace and tone to get it off the ground. "From the very first day," recalls Ann B., "John Rich treated those children like they were responsible, professional actors, and they responded in kind. So when they were supposed to work, they worked. And when they weren't supposed to work, they played or went to school."

Throughout the run of the show, different work schedules were adopted. A five-day schedule changed to four days, and at one point a two-and-a-half day schedule was attempted. Barry remembers, "It was horrendous with all the kids. There was just too much to do. Then we were on a schedule of six days on—Monday to Monday we would work, Tuesday to Tuesday we'd be off, then work Wednesday to Wednesday. Then we would alternate with 'The Odd Couple.' They were next door to us. See, this way, Paramount could only pay one crew. We would do two episodes in three days, then we would be off, and they would do two 'Odd Couples.' Then they went on a completely different work schedule."

As was the standard at the time, the show was shot with one camera on film—in sharp contrast to today's one-inch video tape, multi-camera technique, complete with studio audience! Factoring in the many different sets that had to be lit and dressed, and the number of performers needed for each scene, while abiding by child labor laws, it came down to one thing—a long day, typically ten to twelve hours.

Says Barry, "Filming always began at 8 am for the kids, but what they meant by that was to be *ready* by 8. And being ready means getting there and getting to your dressing room to change into whatever wardrobe there is. After the first or second year a little bit of makeup was used on us to give us that eternal tan look! Then we would go out onto the set and rehearse, and if you weren't doing a scene you'd go right into school."

EDUCATING THE BRADYS: SCHOOL LIFE

To protect the welfare of the child actor, the Los Angeles Unified School District saw not only that the children's scholastic needs were met but that the children were not exploited. A parent or guardian was always to be on the set, and the child was to arrive no earlier than 7 am and work no later than 6 pm, and for no longer than four hours at a time. Children were to receive three hours of studio school daily, in no less than twenty-minute increments. The kids were allotted one hour for lunch, no later than five hours after arrival, and one hour of recreation. Whew! With six children it's a wonder that all this was accomplished!

Mrs. Frances Whitfield was the first of four Brady studio teachers to be employed. A delightful lady, she has since retired from teaching, but her career as a commercial actress still thrives. The other three teachers were Thordis Burkhardt, Shirley Deckert, and Beth Clopton. Remembers Mrs. Whitfield, "We had two schoolrooms. And we had a special arrangement with the Board of Education with what we called bank time, so that if one child was very much featured [on an episode], maybe we had accumulated some time, and we kept a record of that. But it would average to

Susan Olsen flashes the peace sign in studio school.

fifteen hours a week. We never had any occasion to break rules, even if we were on location. . . . All the kids were quite artistic. And they wrote well, Susan particularly. And we had arts and crafts. That corridor was a regular art exhibit!"

If you ever take a tour of the Paramount lot, you may be able to see the remnants of fans' photos and original drawings done by the Bradys that still remain. However, with the daily wear and tear of the stage, not to mention the theft of these artifacts, the images of days gone by are quickly vanishing. Says Susan Olsen, "I was really happy that all my art-work went first. Chris still has a couple of pictures up there. When we were doing 'The Brady Brides,' there was still this picture that I remember so well watching Eve draw. It was of a supermarket, and she designed every label on every product. I almost took it, and I guess I forgot, because the next time I was there it was gone."

In order to minimize disruption of the kids' regular school life, production began in the summer and would go through the winter. "Basically," recalls Barry, "we would spend one semester in studio school and one semester in regular school, but that didn't last long for everyone because it was really tough going back to regular school. I ended up going to a private school and graduated when I was sixteen. It's very difficult to assimilate. You know, kids don't really know how to relate because there's all this attention, so they have a preconception. Social skills aren't very good when you're fourteen or fifteen, so you don't know how to break past that. The whole thing was kind of uncomfortable on a social level. But on a scholastic level it was different because we moved at a different pace. In studio school you can go more quickly because you have one teacher assigned to two or three people. It's a difficult transition, and it's disruptive when you're going in and out."

Says Susan, "I went back to regular [public] school because I was really intent on being normal. It's all in your attitude. It's a very hard thing to go back. You get teased. I used to get a lot of flack for the things Cindy had done—people would think that they couldn't tell me their secrets because Cindy would tattle. Everyone has a preconceived notion of who you are, which you've got to fight. Finally it dawned on me that the kids were jealous. *I* would have been jealous of me if I hadn't been me, so I didn't blame them."

RECREATION, BRADY STYLE

But it wasn't all work and no play. Says Mike Lookinland, "I remember playing on the old 'Bonanza' set. We'd have an hour for lunch and if you have designs on going out to play, it takes you ninety seconds to eat lunch! Me and Chris would play 'Can You Catch Me and Kill Me' kinds of things." Meanwhile, a favorite activity of Susan and Eve's was to feed the "Bonanza" horses. And when they weren't exploring the studio lot, they learned to *needlepoint* from Ann B. Davis. "I taught them all how. For a while we had the boys hooking rugs. They wanted to do something, too, but they didn't want to do *needlepoint*."

Probably the most interesting game involved a meatlocker. Explains Susan, "There was a game we used to play during the first year, before they tore down the old commissary, called, 'Do You Trust Me?' And there was a meatlocker in there and someone would say, 'Do you trust me?' and you'd say, 'Yeah,' and then you would be locked up. The point being that you couldn't get out. Florence's daughter cried once and I don't know if we locked her up and forgot about her or if she freaked out, but it kind of put a stop to our fun!"

The kids became interested in music soon after Sherwood decided to have them sing the opening theme song for the second season. This spawned many "musical" episodes, the production of record albums, and finally, a national touring stint. Somewhere between their school demands and the rigors of production, they all managed to squeeze in daily rehearsals.

One of the most frequently asked questions about the show is, "Did they all get along?" Amazingly, the answer is yes. "These kids all liked each other so much it was almost sickening," Sherwood once said. According to Mike Lookinland, "Believe it or not, we were all good friends. We didn't have the fights you hear about." Eve Plumb agrees: "We weren't allowed to [misbehave]. We were expected to perform as professionals."

Yet another question everyone is eager to resolve is the dating scene between the kids. Barry Williams admits to having dated Maureen McCormick. Christopher Knight went out on a couple of dates with Eve Plumb. Says Christopher, "It sounds strange that we might have dated one another, except, as we grew up, we were who we knew best, and we were around each other more than with our own families." And it appears Barry liked older women, as well. Florence recalls, "Barry and I had a very special rapport. He wasn't able to drive and wasn't yet sixteen, but he wanted to take me out. He's always loved music, so his older brother brought him to my hotel and then I drove my car to the Coconut Grove. Barry was so cute. He even made sure we had a good table. Then he paid the check, I went back to my hotel and his brother picked him up." If you were able to catch the "Geraldo" interview where Florence and Barry recounted this story, you'll remember that it was made to seem as if something more had happened—causing a media uproar. To set the record straight, *nothing happened*. After all, these are the Bradys!

THE BRADY PHENOMENON

The Bradys were—and perhaps still are—the image of what we want or hope to be. Their problems were trivial and were solved in positive ways, and it is this simplicity that has touched a responsive chord. "Kids could identify with the Brady children," explains Sherwood. "A lot of kids who were middle children loved the episode where Jan gets a wig so she can stand out among her sisters [#42, "Will the Real Jan Brady Please Stand Up?"]. We got a lot of mail from these kids who fought that battle. It had enough reality to help whoever needed reassurance. That's the kind of magic that show had. There's nothing wrong with a show that says, 'Hey, I'm not a mirror, I'm maybe better than a mirror.' TV can be more useful as a role model, and I think 'The Brady Bunch' is a role model family." Perhaps the very overidealizing that so disappointed the show's critics is what captured the public's imagination.

This idea of presenting the kids as ones that real children could identify with was foremost in Sherwood's mind during the casting process. "This gets to the heart of a big difference of opinion I had with Paramount," he explains. "At that time the people in development believed in labeling characters in very narrow ways. In other words, they wanted one of the kids to be in love all the time, another kid to be into sports, so that the audience developed a familiarity with that particular kid and his thing. I wanted these kids to be *real* kids. I wanted the kids to determine their own characters. The only thing I wanted for sure was for the oldest boy to be the most responsible, and the same for the oldest girl. Like one of them needed orthodontia and another needed glasses. So these kids gave me their characters and that was pretty much their real personality. Chris Knight was the playboy of the western world, that's just the way he was.

And the tagalong youngest boy was just that. We used reality wherever we could. For example, if the kids were supposed to draw something, we didn't have the propman do it, we'd have the kids do it. I wanted these kids to be real, and I think they *were* real kids."

Adds Barry, "At various times your life can't help but affect the show. One time, just before we were filming an episode, I was in an auto accident and I had a head-on collision—I split my lip almost down to my chin. I went into the set thinking they might have to write me out and they said, 'Hmmm,' and just put a little tiny Band-Aid over it and said, 'Yeah, you cut yourself shaving.' And I said, 'Like with what, a lawn mower?' And that's how we shot the show." (The episode was #110, "Out of This World.")

Nevertheless, there were disputes over exactly what was real. Recalls Susan, "I remember once Maureen was in tears because she had to say 'groovy.' Here she is, a teenager, and she wants to be cool in her real life, and she has to say a word that was already passé. When she asked why, nobody came up with an answer other than 'do it.' But for the most part, they kind of listened. So actually, we were a lot less geeky than we could have been."

All in all, of course, the Bradys were popular whether or not they were "real." So popular, in fact, that a form letter had to be written and sent to families all over the country when kids began sending mail to the show stating they were leaving their families to join the Brady family. Barry at one point received 6,500 fan letters per week! "Brady Bunch" lunchboxes, paper dolls, albums, and fan clubs were also popular. Sherwood believes, however, that Paramount didn't really make full use of the merchandising potential. Today, those "Brady Bunch" collectibles are among the hottest sellers in TV novelty items.

THE FALL OF THE HOUSE OF BRADY

Despite the storm of strongly negative reviews that pursued "The Brady Bunch" throughout its five-season run, the show managed to stay on the air, anchoring ABC's Friday-night prime-time line-up at 8 o'clock. Amazingly, the show never made the top twenty list, but it did fluctuate in the top twenty-to-thirty range in the Nielsen rankings. For a show that appears to its many detractors to be mediocre, it is still staggeringly popular: 70% of all U.S. markets carry the show. It is also syndicated internationally.

In order to win back a much-needed younger audience and thereby boost ratings, Cousin Oliver (Robbie Rist) was brought in as "new blood" in the fifth season. Sherwood says it wasn't his idea, but that he went along with it. At this point, could it hurt? Another idea that was bounced around was the possibility of Carol having twins, but this didn't pan out. That would truly have made Sherwood's original "Yours and Mine" idea into "Yours, Mine and Ours." In any case, the idea would have been unworkable—there wouldn't have been enough squares in the opening grid!

The youth movement failed. "The Brady Bunch" was canceled before the start of the 1974 fall season. Says Sherwood, "[Something] happens after five years. You have to renegotiate everybody's contract, and that's a pain in the neck. Everybody wants super-big raises, and the show at that point was damaged by 'Sanford & Son.' 'Sanford & Son' came on and really hurt the ratings. So, the combination of renegotiation and the fact that we were on a down trend anyway, I kind of knew it was the last of the series. I tried to substitute another show, 'Kelly's Kids' with Brooke Bundy and Ken Berry. It was my idea when 'The Brady Bunch' went off to bring in a new show with a new concept of 'Kelly's Kids' being one white kid, one black kid, and one oriental kid. This is another thing that came out of statistics. An enormous percentage of kids in this country are adopted. I'm always looking for a new way to do things. Just as 'The Brady Bunch' brought together separate families, I felt there were new stories available in adopted kids and their special problems . . . And that's the show I thought was going to replace 'The Brady Bunch,' but it didn't happen." The "Kelly's Kids" "pilot" was actually episode #107, also called "Kelly's Kids," in "The Brady Bunch" series. Ultimately, the short-lived "Kodiak," starring Clint Walker, replaced "The Brady Bunch."

Had the show continued, one thing was certain: Robert Reed would have been replaced. Says Sherwood, "We agreed, Paramount and I, that if there was going to be another year, or years, we would change husbands. Everyone was sick of Bob Reed." There was also the idea of bringing back Carol's first husband. How, you ask? Sherwood explains, "It was never really said that Carol was widowed or divorced. He [husband #1] was 'missing' and was going to have amnesia and come back into her life. It was going to be a major problem." (This idea was also a contender for the later series "The Bradys," but never came to fruition.)

Long before the inception of the successful special "A Very Brady Christmas," a couple of two-hour movies were in the planning stages. One would have taken the family to Italy because of Mike's love of architecture. India was another possibility, with the family involved in some sort of espionage/kidnapping escapade loosely based on Hitchcocks's thriller *The Man Who Knew Too Much.*

Although the original "Brady Bunch" series ended almost twenty years ago, it has probably spawned more direct spin-offs and specials than any other network series in history. The animated "The Brady Kids," a Filmation production, ran on ABC from 1972 to 1974. "The Brady Bunch Variety Hour" (1976) and "The Brady Bunch Hour" (1977), both Sid and Marty Krofft productions, were not, according to Sherwood, authorized by either Sherwood or Paramount. Ultimately, the Kroffts had to pay a royalty. In 1981 Sherwood and his son Lloyd brought "The Brady Brides" to NBC, followed by the highest-rated two-hour movie in 1988, "A Very Brady Christmas." And in 1990 an updated, more realistic version hit the airwaves, "The Bradys," or as Sherwood called it, "Bradysomething."

And on the horizon . . . who knows?

Answers to Rear Cover Quiz

a. Sorry. Marcia made this intimate complaint in episode #63, "Getting Davy Jones."

b. Nope. Episode #110, "Out of This World," featured a close encounter of the Brady kind.

c. Not this one. The boys took it into their head that Sam was working for the Other Side in episode #115, "Top Secret."

d. Congratulations! You remember that Greg only *thought about* pawning the clunker off on his hapless friend Ronnie in episode #53, "The Wheeler Dealer"; in the end, he got the guilts and ultimately commissioned the car to the junkyard. (If you missed this one, maybe it's time you, like Greg, learned a valuable lesson about honesty from Mike.)

e. Wrong. Actually, this question was sneaky. Episode #75, "Today I Am a Freshman," featured a temperamental volcano that spewed forth upon the proceedings—but it was part of Peter's science experiment.

f. Oh, come on! "The Brady Bunch" was a gritty, hard-hitting show in tune with the dawning social, sexual, and cultural changes of the times! (Right.) Anyway, let's just say that *someone* toward the end of the series used this word—and in reference to an encounter with Carol Brady! To find out who, see the final item in "Who Said This?" on page 174. The answer appears upside-down on page 175.

THE ULTIMATE BRADY BUNCH TRIVIA CHALLENGE

Choose the correct answer from the choices listed below.

1. When Cindy wanted to fly like a fairy princess after being cast as one in the school play, what did her brothers do to help?
   a. They hung her up on the clothesline
   b. They threw her out the window
   c. They gave her LSD

2. The grass isn't always greener on the other side, as Mike and Carol learned when they switched roles for the day. While Carol played ball with the boys, what did Mike do with the girls?
   a. He helped them set up a sidewalk lemonade stand
   b. He helped Marcia earn her cooking badge
   c. He made tutus for the girls' ballet recital

3. According to *Teen Time Romance*, one way to achieve a successful marriage is to marry a man ten to twelve years older. What older man did Marcia have in mind?
   a. Sam, the butcher
   b. Davy Jones
   c. Her dentist

4. What did Mike's grandfather do for a living?
   a. He was a UPS driver
   b. He was a judge
   c. He was headmaster of a private boys school

5. Who does Desi Arnaz, Jr., top, according to Marcia?
   a. Chocolate fudge cake with peppermint icing
   b. Captain Kangaroo
   c. Davy Jones

6. What did Alice win for her jingle in the Everpressed Fabric Softener Jingle contest?
   a. A hi-fi stereo set
   b. 2,000 boxes of Everpressed Fabric Softener
   c. A round-trip ticket to Oklahoma City

7. What name did the mad archaeologist give to his tiki totem pole?
   a. Oliver
   b. Sherwood
   c. Pepe

8. What hotel was Davy Jones staying at?
   a. The Holiday Inn in Hollywood
   b. The Helmsley Palace
   c. The Royal Towers Hotel

9. What first made Bobby think Carol was a wicked stepmother?
   a. When she asked him to sweep out the fireplace
   b. When she sent him to his room after he whacked Cindy
   c. When she wouldn't buy him a new bicycle until his birthday

10. When Beebe asked Mike to design her new cosmetics factory, what did she specify?
    a. That it be energy- and cost-efficient
    b. That it be Beebe pink
    c. That he keep their contract confidential

11. When Carol left for the weekend to nurse Aunt Mary, she left
Mike and Alice in charge. What did Alice do?
    a. She slipped on Chinese Checkers left on the living
       room floor and sprained her ankle
    b. She put the make on Mike
    c. She went on strike

12. According to Mike and Carol, how does one become popular?
    a. Only date lettermen and those in the top ten of their
       class
    b. Be yourself
    c. Join every club in school

13. What kind of suits did the Brady men wear circa 1973?
    a. Polyester leisure suits
    b. Polyester hiphugger leisure suits
    c. Polyester hiphugger leisure suits with groovy white
       belts

14. What did Jan use on her face to rid herself of freckles?
    a. Carol's makeup
    b. Lemon juice
    c. Mediterranean sea mud

15. Discussion, eggtimers, and threats wouldn't lower the phone
bill, so Mike took action and did what?
    a. Disconnected the phone
    b. Deducted the calls from the kids' allowance
    c. Installed a payphone in the family room

16. When Mike and Carol went to a costume party, who did they go
as?
    a. Sonny and Cher
    b. Raggedy Ann and Andy
    c. Antony and Cleopatra

17. Who received a tape recorder as a birthday gift?
      a. Bobby
      b. Peter
      c. Cindy

18. What did Alice's military cousin make the Bradys do each morning?
      a. Calisthenics
      b. Salute the flag
      c. Sing the National Anthem

19. Who was the pool shark?
      a. Bobby
      b. Oliver
      c. Sam

20. What was the name of the laundry detergent Carol used before Safe?
      a. Fresh-scent Tide with bleach
      b. Best
      c. White Lye

21. What were Bobby and Cindy looking for when they wandered away from the campsite in the Grand Canyon?
      a. Indians
      b. Dinosaur fossils
      c. Tiger

22. Which kid wanted to be an only child?
      a. Jan
      b. Peter
      c. Cindy

23. What double feature was playing at the drive-in when Bobby accompanied Greg on his date with Rachel?
      a. *Swamp Women* and *Rawhead Rex*
      b. An unnamed western and a science fiction movie
      c. *Eraserhead* and *Brother From Another Planet*

24. What was the name of the rock band formed by Greg's cigarette-smoking friend, Tommy?
   a. The Banana Convention
   b. Three Groovy Guys
   c. The Lettermen

25. When Jan lost her locket, she was leaning out her bedroom window looking at what constellation?
   a. The Big Dipper
   b. The Little Bear
   c. Alpha Centauri

26. What did the Brady boys and girls each want to buy with Alice's Checker Trading stamps?
   a. TV/dollhouse
   b. Rowboat/sewing machine
   c. Camping equipment/vanity

27. What disease did Bobby's girlfriend think she had the day after they kissed?
   a. Shingles
   b. Chicken pox
   c. Mumps

28. Was Dwayne, one of the adopted Kellys:
   a. White
   b. African-American
   c. Asian

29. What did the Brady boys do to ruin the girls' slumber party?
   a. They set off the backyard sprinklers where the girls slept
   b. They invited some of their friends for their own party
   c. They put itching powder in their sleeping bags

30. Which Brady had "Scoop" for a nickname?
    a. Bobby
    b. Peter
    c. Jan

31. When Peter called the hotel where Davy Jones was staying, he told the operator that he was an old friend and part of a famous rock group called:
    a. The Three Desperadoes
    b. Peter, Bobby, and Marcia
    c. The Rescue Rangers

32. When Alice left her job as a result of being called a squealer by the kids, she got a new job as:
    a. A waitress at the Golden Spoon Cafe
    b. A bank teller for the Valley Community Bank
    c. An apprentice butcher with Sam

33. What does the Bradys' neighbor, Mr. Kelly, do for a living?
    a. He does a nightclub act
    b. He's a partner in Mike's firm
    c. He owns a Taco Bell franchise

34. At 10:00 pm the Bunch reenacted the previous night's events in order to find Jan's lost locket. Bobby was brushing his teeth, Cindy was in the hall, Peter and Greg were raiding the fridge, and Alice was writing her sister. What was Marcia doing?
    a. She was on the phone with a friend
    b. She got jealous of Jan getting a mysterious locket and chucked it out the window
    c. She was studying for an English test in bed

35. Who's older?
    a. Tiger
    b. Bobby

36. What famous trio did the Kelly kids associate themselves with?
    a. Moe, Larry, and Curly
    b. The Three Musketeers
    c. The Del Rubio triplets

37. What was the name of gold prospector Zaccariah T. Brown's mule?
    a. Eeyore
    b. Bessie
    c. Samantha

38. What was a boyfriend of Marcia's interested in?
    a. Wacky packs
    b. Baseball cards
    c. Bugs

39. Who sponsored the "Father Of The Year" essay contest?
    a. *Teen Time Romance* magazine
    b. Mr. Sanders, the school's principal
    c. The *Daily Chronicle* newspaper

40. Who broke the bust of Mike that Carol had sculpted?
    a. Alice
    b. Sam
    c. Mike

41. Which letter was dropped in the typewritten envelope addressed to Jan in the lost locket episode?
    a. Y
    b. R
    c. A

42. Davy Jones accompanied Marcia:
    a. To the Junior Prom
    b. On a date to Harry's Hogie Hut
    c. To Senior Banquet Night

43. When the Bradys built a dunking booth for the school carnival, who accidentally got dunked?
    a. Alice
    b. Bobby
    c. Mike

44. Why did Marcia fire Peter from the ice cream parlor?
    a. Because he goofed off too much
    b. Because he worked harder and threatened her job security
    c. Because he gave his friends free ice cream

45. Where did Mike and Carol hang the photo the kids gave them for their anniversary?
    a. Over the fireplace in the living room
    b. In the family room
    c. In their bedroom

46. What book was Cindy reading to make herself appear older?
    a. *The Catcher In The Rye*
    b. *The Other Side Of Midnight*
    c. *A Farewell To Arms*

47. Mike said Tiger couldn't go to the wedding, and made the boys put him back in the car. How did Tiger get out?
    a. He lowered the electric window button with his paw and jumped out
    b. Bobby felt it wasn't fair that the girls' cat got to be there and Tiger couldn't so he let him out
    c. His barking was disrupting the wedding so Mike let him out after all

48. Why was Jerry Rogers, Fairview High's star football player, dating Marcia?
    a. Because she was groovy
    b. Because he wanted to steal Greg's playbook
    c. Because she was head cheerleader

49. What was the name of the baseball team Greg and Peter played on?
    a. The Rockets
    b. The Smogdogs
    c. The Aces

50. Who wrote an essay entitled, "The Importance Of Choosing A Career?"
    a. Marcia
    b. Greg
    c. Peter

51. Who was going to be guest of honor at Marcia's Senior Banquet Night?
    a. An astronaut
    b. A senator
    c. A pop music idol

52. When Mike went to talk to Buddy Hinton's father about Buddy's bullying Cindy, what happened?
    a. Mike came away with a black eye
    b. Mike walked away and taught Peter how to fight
    c. Mike beat him up

53. For Family Frolics Night, what was the name of the poem Mike read?
    a. "The Raven" by Edgar Allen Poe
    b. "The Day Is Done" by Henry Wadsworth Longfellow
    c. "The Waste Land" by T.S. Eliot

54. Which Christmas carol did Carol sing in church?
    a. "Silent Night"
    b. "Rudolph The Red-Nosed Reindeer"
    c. "O Come, All Ye Faithful"

55. What conflicted with Peter's football practice?
    a. Glee Club
    b. Ballet
    c. Band practice

56. Sam and Alice got into a squabble over what to give their friend as a wedding gift. What romantic idea did Sam have in mind?
    a. Finger chalk
    b. A meat grinder
    c. His and hers bowling balls

57. On Alice and Sam's first date, what did Sam give her and where did they go?
    a. A dozen red roses and to the ballet
    b. Porkchops and to Antonio's Italian Restaurant
    c. An orchid and bowling

58. What part did Bobby and Peter play in the film Greg made for a class project?
    a. Aliens
    b. Confederate/Union soldiers
    c. American Indians

59. What did Greg leave the football team to become?
    a. Johnny Bravo
    b. A yell leader
    c. The official photographer

60. Who rescued Cindy from Buddy Hinton, the school bully?
    a. Peter
    b. Bobby
    c. Tiger

61. When Mike drove Marcia to the set of "The Hank Coleman Show," where Davy Jones was appearing as a guest, they were told that the show was taped a day in advance. Who was the guest that day?
    a. The Professor, via satellite from Gilligan's Island
    b. The head of the Department of Sanitation
    c. Tiny Tim

62. Why was Marcia sick the first day of high school?
    a. Because she had a zit
    b. Because she was afraid
    c. Because she partied hard the night before

63. How was it determined who won Alice's Checker Trading stamps?
    a. A domino game
    b. A cardhouse game
    c. A treasure hunt

64. Which Brady had laryngitis?
    a. Carol
    b. Cindy
    c. Peter

65. What kind of food item did Carol and Alice both make for the charity hoedown?
    a. Chili
    b. Cheese blintzes
    c. Strawberry preserves

66. Who was going to make a million dollars selling "Neat and Natural" hair tonic?
    a. Cindy
    b. Bobby
    c. Oliver

67. What happened to the pool table?
   a. It was stolen
   b. Mike couldn't make the payments so it was repossessed
   c. Mike gave it to charity because they had no room for it

68. How did Mike know that the picture of the kids he and Carol got was not the original?
   a. Because the photographer called him to pay for another print
   b. Because the kids were in a different order
   c. Because Jan was wearing her glasses

69. Why did Cindy dress as Shirley Temple?
   a. Because she read in Marcia's diary that she had a chance to be discovered as the next Shirley Temple
   b. Because she had the lead role in the school production of *Little Miss Marker*
   c. As a Halloween costume

70. What was the excuse Alice gave Carol for resigning after being labled a squealer by the kids?
   a. She had to help her Uncle Winston run his dress shop
   b. She needed a break in routine
   c. Cindy got on her nerves

71. Who's on top? (In the opening grid, that is.)
   a. Mike
   b. Carol

72. What did the Brady girls ultimately buy with the Checker Trading Stamps?
   a. A sewing machine
   b. A swingset
   c. A color television

73. Mom said "Don't play ball in the house," but that didn't stop Peter. What broke as a result of a runaway basketball?
    a. A model of the city courthouse Mike built
    b. Carol's favorite vase
    c. A bust of Mike

74. Which Brady or Bradys needed a tonsilectomy?
    a. Carol and Cindy
    b. Bobby
    c. Tiger

75. Who erased Alice's recipe from the blackboard?
    a. Peter, to demonstrate a football play
    b. Carol, to write down the shopping list
    c. Greg, to write down a chick's phone number

76. Was Steve, one of the Kellys' adopted children:
    a. Asian
    b. American Indian
    c. African-American

77. With what did Bobby bribe his friend Tommy to play Cindy's secret admirer?
    a. A silver dollar
    b. A lizard
    c. A kazoo

78. Where did the Bradys stop on their way to the Grand Canyon?
    a. Las Vegas
    b. Cactus Creek Ghost Town
    c. King's Island Amusement Park

79. Why did Bobby and Oliver lock Sam in the meat locker?
    a. To protect him from thugs who were looking for their payback
    b. Because they thought he was a spy for the Russians
    c. Because he dumped Alice

80. Plagued by bad luck, the boys decide to return the tiki idol to the ancient burial grounds where they meet:
    a. Professor Hubert Whitehead, a mad archeologist
    b. The Sleestacks
    c. Mr. Hanalei, the Hawaiian folklorist

81. Was Matt, one of the adopted Kelly children:
    a. White
    b. African-American
    c. Asian

82. What kind of football injury did Greg have?
    a. A hairline fracture of the ribs
    b. A sprained ankle
    c. An out of joint shoulder

83. What were the names of Sam's bowling teams?
    a. The Meatmen and the Butchers
    b. The Bowling Bolonies and the Beefsteaks
    c. The Meatpackers and the Meatcutters

84. Where did Mike and Carol's grandparents elope to?
    a. Hawaii
    b. Las Vegas
    c. South Korea

85. Why wouldn't Cindy tell her folks what happened to the registered letter Alice received?
    a. Because she forgot
    b. Because she was angry at Alice for squealing on her
    c. Because she didn't want Tiger to go to Siberia

86. Greg wanted a car, so he took a job as a messenger boy at Mike's company—but he was fired after his first day. Why?
    a. Because he lost Mike's plans at a newsstand while looking at car magazines
    b. Because he was late
    c. Because he made lousy coffee

87. When Beebe visited the Brady house, what happened?
   a. She was the unintentional target of a toy airplane and squirt gun fire
   b. The green-eyed monster got hold of Carol, who whacked her
   c. Cindy, thinking Beebe was a talent agent, performed her Shirley Temple act

88. What did Jan's "soul sister" give her as a gift?
   a. A portrait of herself
   b. A pair of love birds
   c. A locket

89. What was the name of the song Davy Jones sang?
   a. "Girl"
   b. "Kumbaya"
   c. "Puff, The Magic Dragon"

90. After Mike brought home an old dilapidated rowboat to be given to the junkyard, the Bradys fixed it up and called it:
   a. The Brady Boat
   b. The S.S. Brady
   c. The Boatmobile

91. Who sent Jan the locket?
   a. Aunt Jenny
   b. Alice
   c. Sam

92. Like Batman and Robin, what was the first thing the Bradys did whenever they got in the car?
   a. Got out the sing-along book
   b. Fastened their seatbelts
   c. Lit up a cigarette

93. After the Bradys spent the first day of their camping trip together, what did they feast on for dinner?
    a. Quiche
    b. Coldcuts, cheese, and fried chicken
    c. Fresh trout

94. When the Bradys planned a ski vacation, which Brady was not included, and why?
    a. Jan, because she wanted privacy
    b. Peter, because he broke Carol's favorite vase
    c. Marcia, because she was caught outside late at night

95. Tiger temporarily left the Bradys because:
    a. Peter left the backyard gate open and he got lost
    b. He went to look after his new wife and puppies
    c. Robbers kidnapped him

96. "Sherlock Peter" was hired by Cindy to find what?
    a. Carol's earrings
    b. Greg's mouse
    c. Kitty Karry-All

97. Why did the washing machine overflow?
    a. Because Bobby got his good suit dirty while rescuing a runaway cat, and in trying to clean it before the folks got home, he dumped the whole box of detergent in the machine
    b. While Alice and Sam were making out in the laundry room, Sam accidentally knocked the box of detergent into the machine and it started up
    c. Cindy got bored with taking baths and decided to try the machine out for a change

98. What dinner did Marcia fix to earn her cooking badge?
    a. Goose confit with strawberry-rhubarb sauce
    b. Macaroni and cheese, and jello for dessert
    c. Chilled tomato juice with lemon, veal cutlets, green beans, and cake with chocolate icing

99. Which of the Brady kids wore braces?
        a. Cindy, Bobby, Jan and Marcia
        b. No one
        c. Peter

100. What Hawaiian celebrity did the Bradys meet?
        a. Jack Lord
        b. King Kamehameha
        c. Don Ho

Answers

1. a	26. b	51. a	76. a
2. b	27. c	52. b	77. a
3. c	28. b	53. b	78. b
4. b	29. c	54. c	79. b
5. b	30. b	55. a	80. a
6. a	31. a	56. c	81. a
7. a	32. a	57. c	82. a
8. c	33. a	58. c	83. c
9. a	34. c	59. c	84. b
10. b	35. a	60. a	85. c
11. a	36. b	61. b	86. a
12. b	37. b	62. b	87. a
13. c	38. c	63. b	88. a
14. b	39. c	64. a	89. a
15. c	40. a	65. c	90. b
16. c	41. a	66. b	91. b
17. b	42. a	67. c	92. b
18. a	43. a	68. c	93. b
19. a	44. a	69. a	94. c
20. b	45. c	70. a	95. b
21. b	46. c	71. b	96. a
22. a	47. a	72. c	97. a
23. b	48. b	73. b	98. c
24. a	49. a	74. a	99. a
25. b	50. b	75. a	100. c

WHO SAID THIS?

DIRECTIONS: Which character—Mike, Carol, Alice, Sam, Marcia, Jan, Cindy, Greg, Peter, Bobby, or Oliver—authored or spoke the words below?

1. Caveat emptor!

2. Cold cuts, cheese, salami, fried chicken! We might as well camp in a supermarket!

3. My beautiful little locket. No card or return address. Gone, as mysteriously as it came.

4. And every time I see him on television I just feel, wow, Desi Arnaz, Jr.! He's *so cute*! And my dream of dreams is to be Mrs. Desi Arnaz, Jr. Until tomorrow . . .

5. Eenie, Meenie, Mommy, Daddy.

6. I'm going to be a baseball player. They don't have to know anything—I mean, except for baseball.

7. Effective immediately, we all share, and share alike!

8. Mom, Mom! I won, I won! I'm gonna be on television!

9. I am a little sunflower,
   Sunny, brave, and true.
   From tiny bud to blossom
   I do good deeds for you.

10. I've got a secret, I've got a secret. It's for me to know and you to find out!

11. When I think of your face and your awful cute dimples
    From head to toe I get goose pimples.

12. For the fabrics that are best
    Put your faith in Everpressed
    You will always look well-dressed
    And you never will be messed. Up.

13. The best dog in the world was lost today and we want him back.

14. Oh mom, not glasses, I'll look positively goofy!

15. Well, I don't want any more help. I'm getting helped right out of everything I wanna do. I want to write my own screenplay, design my own sets, choose my costumes, and pick the actors. Don't you see, it's my project! It has to be my work. I'm the only one who gets graded on it. And if I can't do it, then the movie's off. And that's what it is, off!

16. I got my job back, Mr. Foster, and I'm never gonna leave it again.

17. All I hear all day long at school is how great Marcia is at this or how wonderful Marcia did that. Marcia. Marcia, Marcia, Marcia!

18. Dr. Stanley Vogel. Oh you should see him. He is far out. He has dark gorgeous hair, dreamy eyes, groovy bell-bottom pants, neat shoes, and he plays rock 'n' roll music in his office!

19. Dear Friends: Thank you for giving me this honor. But even more important than winning was a lesson I've learned. It has to do with being grateful, of giving and receiving. Well, I'm very grateful. I've received and now, I'm going to start giving. In the campaign, making promises just to get elected is wrong. And if it takes me the rest of my life, I'm going to keep every promise I've made to everybody.

20. Oh, my nose!

21. It seems to me you're a bad winner. You know, you shouldn't put down a loser, Cindy, because you might be one yourself one day. Just remember that.

22. I'm in high school now, and when you're in high school your're not a kid anymore, you're a man. And a man doesn't want to be pestered by kids. He wants privacy.

23. Something suddenly came up!

24. Television stars don't play in teepees, and they don't get dirty!

25. I'm not going to wear any skirt, and I'm not going to sell any cookies!

26. Every guy in my class is okay except one—Warren Mulaney. As far as I'm concerned he's public enemy number one. I guess you guys didn't hear that he beat me out on the first string basketball team. The guy's on the top of my crumb list, in fact, he's on the bottom on my crumb list, too, and he's every crumb in between!

27. Well, I kinda bugged the rooms with Dad's tape recorder.

28. I could make the decision for you, but it wouldn't be right. I would like to give you something to think about, though. You know, money and fame are very important things, but, well, sometimes there are other things that are important—like people.

29. I bet you a million dollars you can't do twice as many chin-ups as I can!

30. You don't ask a boy to call you, you get them to call you by being mature . . . playing it cool.

31. Well, tonight's the semi-finals of the Supermarket Bowling League. Us Meatcutters against the Bread and Pastry Boys.

32. You made him disappear just like that lady, and he's never coming back! Mommy, Mommy, Peter made Bobby disappear!

33. Look, I've taken out the trash for you, and I hosed off the patio, I shined your shoes, I made your bed, cleaned your bike, I even let you beat me at checkers 'cause you told me to. But that's it, that's it, understand? It didn't include taking you on dates!

34. I'll show him, Alice! Women can be better drivers than men. Men are egotistical, arrogant, smug, and conceited!

35. Oh Alice! With all that hardware on your head you punctured your air mattress.

36. You don't have to pretend anymore. I know all about the talent thcout who's coming over here tonight to see me . . . I got to confess—I peeked in your diary and I know everything. That client Dad's talking about is really the anonymouth talent thcout.

37. Oh no! Tomorrow's graduation and I've got orange hair!

38. You know, he said you are what you think you are, so from now on I'm beautiful and noble—I'm Juliet!

39. I've never been so humiliated in my whole life—I froze at the wheel!

40. Alice's face is my inspiration. Why, I see her face in every bowling ball, her figure in every bowling pin.

41. Listen Mr. Chin-up King, I've done everything you've asked fair and square. But there's no way, no way are you going on my date with Rachel!

42. So it sticks a little. Listen, when you've got a convertible, who uses doors? You just kinda jump in like it's a sports car, right? Watch this . . .

43. I'm delighted to meet you boys. It's so beneficial for me to be away from those children in junior high, and to be with people of my own mature growth. I'm looking forward to the intellectual stimulation.

44. Oh no! Mike's head!

45. Watch it—I can also cite you for arguing with a safety monitor.

46. I'll tell you what the problem is. You have to wait in line for everything around here. Someone's always borrowing your things. I never have any privacy because I've got too many brothers and sisters. I wish I were an only child!

47. I'm burning up. I've got to get out. I must have air, give me air.

48. All I'm asking you to do is hide in the bushes like Cyrano did, and you feed me the right words. When it comes to small talk and girls, everyone says you're the greatest!

49. I'm a jinx!

50. I hate high school! I hate it, I hate it!

51. Porkchooops and applesauce.

52. But I want to be George Washington!

53. I think it's unfair for you to ground me when I didn't disobey you . . . If you had said *not to drive* for a week, that would have meant *any* car . . . You said not to drive *our* car!

54. My Mexican dinner comes in three degrees: hot, very hot, and pass the fire extinguisher!

55. My diary—in a used bookstore. My most private, most personal emotions. Naked, on public display, for anyone to see.

56. Oh, Mike!

57. Now everyone's got a trophy except for me. I'll never win at anything.

58. Young lady, pick up that receiver and put it down properly!

59. Rachel, you are the greatest, grooviest, most understanding person in the whole world!

60. Fellas, I'm no squealer. My mouth is shut!

61. Hi, Millicent. I have to make sure of something—whether it's skyrockets or not.

62. Tonight's the night. Our big double date. Boy, an older woman!

63. I have the sniffles, but I can blow my own nose.

64. We have a wonderful bunch of kids. I mean really marvelous. They don't play hooky, they don't lie, they're not fresh. But, boy, they just won't stay off that phone!

65. If I can't be a wacky dwarf, I'll be a wicked witch! Ha, ha, ha, ha!

66. You might as well know. If I'm not Priscilla, I'm not going to be in your dumb old movie!

67. Hey, wait a minute, wait a minute! I got it! Oh boy, is this beautiful! Itching powder in their sleeping bags!

68. Well, I finished my classwork a little early and I was doodling and my name happened to be on the paper. I was doodling George Washington, I didn't doodle Mrs. Denton!

69. Do you have any kind of um, well . . . something to get rid of freckles? It's for a friend of mine.

70. I'm looking for a wig.

71. He's not my "little friend" from school. He's taller than I am and he's the best-looking boy in my class. You came in there on purpose just to turn on your icky old charm!

72. Theven thilver thwans thwam thilently theaward.

73. Reasoning. Calm, cool reasoning. That's a lot better than violence. And it's the only sensible way to settle differences.

74. I can't talk!

75. Okay, that settles it. I'm modernizing my meat locker!

76. We're going to start a new teeter-totter record, okay Mom?

77. Okay, once again kids, I've called a late evening meeting. But this time it's not to issue a medical bulletin or to lecture you about carelessness. It's to tell you how proud I am and how pleased that you've gotten together and worked as a team!

78. You asked me what Harvey likes, and that's what Harvey likes. Bugs!

79. Mom, Dad! It happened, it happened! I got my first job, I'm going to fix bikes!

80. All right, if you don't want to come to my party, you don't have to come. I've invited a lot of other friends anyway. And it's gonna be real swell, whether any of my brothers or sisters are there or not!

81. I want to join the Frontier Scouts.

82. You know something, Alice? You've got a bigger heart than a cow!

83. I'll show 'em. I'm not going to stay where I'm not wanted. I'm gonna run away. That's what I'm gonna do, run away.

84. Look, man, the book's a phony.

85. Two o'clock and all is well, and no strange women have come into my life yet!

86. Daddy, Daddy! Thanta's going to give Mommy her voith back for Chrithmath!

87. I'm not a snitcher! I just tell it like it is!

88. Thee thells thea thells by the thea thore.

89. Let's go ahead with it. If Rome can outlast an invasion by the barbarians, what can a few little girls do to the Brady house?

90. I can't do it! I can't hand out punishments . . . I'm the one who busted the vase!

91. Like, you see Dad . . . These clothes, they're too straight for high school . . . It's that in high school, well, like, clothes are really important.

92. And boy, is Greg ever a great driver! We just missed getting into an accident . . . You see, there was this great big truck in front of us and Greg slammed on the breaks and we skidded right in between the big truck and the freeway fence! Honest Dad, he wasn't driving too fast. He just bought a new record album. He was looking at the back cover.

93. And now, watch the lava ooze out!

94. Call back Mr. Crawford and explain why I was discussing a multi-million dollar deal and couldn't deposit another ten cents?

95. I think I'll send Aunt Jenny a picture of myself and ask her to send me a picture of herself. I can hardly wait to see what she looks like!

96. Mom, Dad! It worked, it worked! I grew a whole inch and a half!

97. The talent thcout's coming over here this evening anonymouthly! I have to buy a Shirley Temple record album! I've got to start being Shirley Temple right away!

98. Carol. Carol. Caaaaarrrrooooooooool!?!

99. Now listen, Alice. You can holler about my always being late, gripe about the high prices of my meat, hate my neckties, but when it comes to bowling, you've gotta have a little respect!

100. You know something, Cindy? I think your Mom has a problem discussing sex.

1. Mike	26. Greg	51. Peter	76. Bobby
2. Greg	27. Peter	52. Peter	77. Mike
3. Jan	28. Carol	53. Greg	78. Marcia
4. Marcia	29. Bobby	54. Alice	79. Peter
5. Cindy	30. Marcia	55. Marcia	80. Peter
6. Greg	31. Sam	56. Carol	81. Marcia
7. Mike	32. Cindy	57. Bobby	82. Sam
8. Cindy	33. Greg	58. Mike	83. Bobby
9. Peter	34. Marcia	59. Greg	84. Greg
10. Cindy	35. Mike	60. Alice	85. Mike
11. Bobby	36. Cindy	61. Bobby	86. Cindy
12. Alice	37. Greg	62. Peter	87. Cindy
13. Bobby	38. Marcia	63. Cindy	88. Cindy
14. Jan	39. Marcia	64. Mike	89. Mike
15. Greg	40. Sam	65. Alice	90. Peter
16. Alice	41. Greg	66. Jan	91. Greg
17. Jan	42. Greg	67. Greg	92. Bobby
18. Marcia	43. Marcia	68. Marcia	93. Peter
19. Jan	44. Carol	69. Jan	94. Mike
20. Marcia	45. Bobby	70. Jan	95. Jan
21. Carol	46. Jan	71. Jan	96. Bobby
22. Greg	47. Marcia	72. Cindy	97. Cindy
23. Marcia	48. Peter	73. Mike	98. Mike
24. Cindy	49. Oliver	74. Carol	99. Sam
25. Peter	50. Marcia	75. Sam	100. Oliver

Answers

MISTAKES THAT SLIPPED PAST

In "The Honeymoon" (#0, pilot), take a close look when Tiger rolls down the window with the electric window button. Notice the *manual* window handle in the shot.

In "Kitty Karry-All Is Missing" (#2) Bobby strolls into the family room tooting his kazoo and finds Cindy on the couch disconsolate over the loss of her doll. A few minutes later Bobby discovers that his kazoo is missing and accuses Cindy of stealing it. Mike comes in and gives one of his lectures, then Carol walks in and declares, "I wish I had better news to report. I searched the house again—no doll, no kazoo." How could she have known that the kazoo was missing?

In "54-40 And Fight" (#11) keep your eye on Jan's hair when they're building the house of cards. It's up in a pony-tail in one angle, and down in another. Also, towards the end of the scene, watch how Marcia holds her arm when she's adding another card. In one angle she's holding her bracelet, and in another it dangles. Finally, when the cards fall, there are two cards that still stand (they were rigged with wires). Mike goes over to the table and pushes them down *twice*, but they pop back up again!

In "What Goes Up . . ." (#36) Florence Henderson mistakenly says "Hey, go get 'em, Chris!" when *Peter* is jumping on the trampoline.

This is followed by two mistakes from Barry Williams. First, while Eve ("Jan Brady") Plumb is bouncing, he says, "Be careful, Eve!" soon followed by, "Why don't you give it a try, Eve?" This last statement makes absolutely no sense anyway, since "Jan" had already had her turn—an editing slip, I guess.

In "The Winner" (#46) Mike and Carol take Bobby to the "Kartoon King" show in the blue convertible, but come back in the brown wagon.

Of "Cindy Brady, Lady" (#67) Susan Olsen says: "I was having a hard time remembering my lines that day and I thought we were still rehearsing. After Tommy greets me at the door, I come into the kitchen with a bouquet of flowers and hand them to Alice. As I'm walking out, I make a face." She stuck out her tongue, but the scene was used anyway.

In "The Bradys" episode #4, "Hat In The Ring," Mike's middle name is incorrect. When sworn in as City Councilman, he is called Michael *Thomas* Brady. His correct name is Michael *Paul* Brady, per the pilot episode, "The Honeymoon." And don't think this slip went unnoticed. Sherwood Schwartz's office received dozens of letters!

BRADY NEPOTISM

Over the years, many real-life Brady relatives appeared on the show. Some had guest starring roles, while others were mere extras. Most notable include:

In "The Slumber Caper" (#30), three of the girls invited to Marcia's slumber party are Brady relations: Jenny is Hope Sherwood (Sherwood Schwartz's daughter), Karen is Carolyn Reed (Robert Reed's daughter) and

Hope Sherwood, daughter of producer Sherwood Schwartz, proves that relatives get no special treatment in episode #65, "The Big Bet."

Ruthie is Barbara Henderson (Florence Henderson's daughter).

In "The Big Bet" (#65) Hope Sherwood makes her second appearance—and her first as Rachel, Greg's favorite drive-in date.

In "The Show Must Go On??" (#81) Frank DeVol, the show's musical director, plays the saxophone as part of Family Night Frolics.

In "You Can't Win 'Em All" (#82) Edward Knight (Christopher Knight's father) plays Monty Marshall, the host of "Question The Kids."

In "Everyone Can't Be George Washington" (#85) Peggy is played by Barbara Bernstein, the second appearance by Florence Henderson's daughter.

In "Greg Gets Grounded" (#89) Hope Sherwood makes her third

appearance, and her second as Greg's girlfriend Rachel.

In "Snow White & The Seven Bradys" (#95) the Bradys stage a backyard play to raise money for a retirement gift for "Mrs. Whitfield," Cindy's teacher. In real life, Mrs. Whitfield *was* the Brady kids' studio teacher and social worker.

In "The Cincinnati Kids" (#102) that's producer Lloyd Schwartz, Sherwood Schwartz's son, in the bear costume!

In "Kelly's Kids" (#107) Matt is played by Mike Lookinland's brother, Todd.

In "Out of This World" (#110) the Kaplutians were played by little people, Frank and Sadie Delfino, who acted as stunt doubles for Mike Lookinland and Susan Olsen throughout the series run.

In "Welcome Aboard" (#112) that's Lloyd Schwartz again, clapping the slate for the slapstick scene featuring the Bradys.

In "The Hair-Brained Scheme" (#116) Barbara Bernstein and Hope Sherwood make their last appearances as Greg's classmates, whom he runs into at the beauty salon.

In "The Brady Girls Get Married" the organist at Marcia and Jan's wedding is Karen Lookinland, Mike Lookinland's mother.

In "A Very Brady Christmas" Mrs. Whitfield, the Bradys kids' studio teacher, appears once again. She plays Amy the nurse. However, she is credited as Frances Louise Turner, her maiden name. Florence Henderson's assistant, Patricia Mullins, plays the receptionist. Barbara Mallory, Lloyd Schwartz's wife, plays Mrs. Powell, the lady in labor.

Little people Frank and Sadie Delfino (episode #110, "Out of This World") with Mike Lookinland.

In "The Bradys" two hour debut, "Start Your Engines" (#1) and "Here We Grow Again" (#2), Barbara Mallory reprises her role as Mrs. Powell. Hope (Sherwood) Juber plays Erica Hopkins.

In "A Moving Experience" ("The Bradys," #3) Florence Henderson's assistant, Patricia Mullins, plays Joan, the secretary.

In "Hat In The Ring" ("The Bradys," #4) the show's musical director, Frank DeVol, appears as Man #2.

THE GRAND CANYON QUIZ

DIRECTIONS: Match each family member with his or her appointed Indian name from episode #51, "The Brady Braves."

1. Mike
2. Carol
3. Greg
4. Peter
5. Bobby
6. Marcia
7. Jan
8. Cindy
9. Alice

a. Wandering Blossom
b. Dove At Morning Light
c. Middle Buffalo/Sleeping Lizard
d. Stalking Wolf
e. Big Eagle of Large Nest
f. Little Bear Who Loses Way
g. Willow Dancing in Wind
h. Yellow Flower With Many Petals
i. Squaw-In-Waiting

Answers

9. i	6. g	3. d
8. a	5. f	2. h
7. b	4. c	1. e

WHAT'S MY NAME, Part 1

DIRECTIONS: Match the left column to the correct correlation on the right.

1. Mike's ex-belle	a. Franklin
2. Temporary housekeeper	b. Dittmeyers
3. Bully	c. Beebe Gallini
4. Bobby's first love	d. Molly Webber
5. "Pink" cosmetic queen	e. Martin
6. Sam's last name	f. Dr. Vogel
7. Mike's boss	g. Kellys
8. Alice's ex-WAC cousin	h. Buddy Hinton
9. Next door neighbors	i. Millicent
10. Indian boy	j. Jimmy Pakaya
11. One-time wallflower	k. Mr. Phillips
12. Carol's grandmother	l. Connie Hutchins
13. Neighbors who adopted three kids	m. Kay
14. Dentist Marcia fell for	n. Emma
15. Carol's previous married name	o. Bobo

Answers

15. e	10. j	5. c
14. f	9. b	4. i
13. g	8. n	3. h
12. l	7. k	2. m
11. d	6. a	1. o

WHAT'S MY NAME, Part 2

DIRECTIONS: Match the left column to the correct correlation on the right.

1. Herlo and Shim
2. Tami Cutler
3. Mr. Hanalei
4. Harvey Klinger
5. Penelope Fletcher
6. Dwayne, Matt and Steve
7. Fender bender man
8. Alice's swindler boyfriend
9. Ice cream parlor owner
10. Marcia's first boyfriend
11. Safe soap acting coach
12. Bike shop owner
13. High school boy Marcia dated and Greg hated
14. Carol's maiden name
15. Carol's ex-beau

a. Bug enthusiast
b. Adoptees
c. Music agent
d. Mark Millard
e. Alan Anthony
f. Tank Gates
g. Tyler
h. Warren Mulaney
i. Aliens
j. Myrna Carter
k. Cultural center lady
l. Mr. Martinelli
m. Hawaiian folklorist
n. Mr. Haskell
o. Harry Duggan

Answers

15. f	10. e	5. k
14. g	9. n	4. a
13. h	8. d	3. m
12. l	7. o	2. c
11. j	6. b	1. i

PART THREE

MUCH MORE THAN
A HUNCH

Spinoffs and Tributes

BRADY BUNCH COLLECTIBLES

Attention, all Brady fans! If you're into collectibles, here's the most complete list in existence of "Brady Bunch" merchandise from its heyday and beyond. Of course, you'll really have to scrounge around flea markets, yard sales, toy trade magazines, and private sales to find any of these items. If you already are a proud owner, hold on to whatever you have. The items are actually worth something, and their value is increasing.

Erin and Don Smith's collection . . .

Just about everything you can imagine was produced with the Brady Bunch name attached to it—from the quality (whatever that is) albums, paperbacks, View-Master sets, and paper dolls, to the cheap and cheesy dimestore realm of the Brady Bunch Toy Tea Set, Fishin' Fun, Magic Slate, and Banjo. Anything for a buck, I guess.

Of all of it, the lunch box seems to be the most sought-after

. . . and Johnnie J. Young's.

item. It was designed by Nick LoBionco, who also created the Monkees' guitar logo. The front side depicts the wedding scene, and the back is

Collect 'em all!

taken from episode #12, "A Camping We Will Go."

One of the rarest of Brady finds is the Topps Chewing Gum eighty-eight-card set. In 1971 the full set of eighty-eight cards was issued, after a "test run" of fifty-five cards. Although there is no significant difference between cards one through fifty-five as they appear in each series, you *can* determine which category your card falls into by checking the copyright date on the back. Now stay with me on this one—the 1970 test run cards have the appropriate 1970 date, but the 1971 eighty-eight-card set is dated 1969. This refers to the *original* licensing date of the full set. When Topps decided to put out the test run they needed an additional copyright.

Trick or treat!

The Halloween costume merits a special mention for sheer ridiculousness. The box boasts, "The Brady Bunch (Greg)—costume plus mask." The "costume," however, turns out to be a two-color silkscreen smock that says, "One of the Brady Bunch," and the mask was simply a red Lone Ranger-style mask—no sign of Greg. Research indicates that no actual character masks were ever made. To add to the confusion, the costume has a 1969 copyright, but the picture on the smock is from the 1972 "Meet The Brady Bunch" album cover. Hmm.

Regarding apparel, Sherwood says, "I know that I was very angry because Paramount couldn't make a deal with a clothing company that wanted to put out Brady dresses and jeans. I think those would have been big sellers."

Greg's Johnny Bravo suit—for sale?!

THE MUSICAL BUNCH

Having seen the success of "The Partridge Family," the Bradys didn't take long to jump on the musical bandwagon. Their first album, "Merry Christmas From The Brady Bunch," took only two weeks to crank out, with the kids credited as their TV pseudonyms. ("Marcia," by the way, is misspelled on the jacket: "Marsha.") Interestingly, seasoned vocalist and family matriarch Florence Henderson was not asked to participate. A point of frustration, to say

the least; so much so, in fact, that she developed a singing act of her own with her real-life children—called The Bernstein Bunch. Paramount ran interference, however, and it never came to be. So if you want her rendition of "O Come, All Ye Faithful," you'll have to tape it off the tube.

With "Merry Christmas" out, Barry wanted to embark on a solo career of his own and talked Paramount's music division, Famous Music, into a record contract. "We recorded six out of the eleven songs I was going to do, but Paramount decided that if one Brady was good, six would be better, so they effectively refused to release mine and started making those Brady albums, which, of course, speak for themselves!"

The second and third of "those Brady albums," "Meet the Brady Bunch" and "The Kids From The Brady Bunch" were produced by Jackie Mills, known for his work with Davy Jones and Bobby Sherman. The tracks were a combination of catchy popular tunes of the day, such as "American Pie," and original tunes written especially for the series. The instrumentation and back-up vocalists were prerecorded, and most of the time it's hard to tell which party is actually singing backup! (Incidentally, some of the same backup vocalists sang on the Partridge Family albums.) A few of the key tracks—"Time To Change," "It's A Sunshine Day," and

"Keep On"—were featured on episodes #64, "Dough Re Mi," and #92, "Amateur Nite," among the best known and loved in the series. The kids performed as the Brady Six in the former, and as The Silver Platters in the latter. (Remember that choreography? Truly, TV at its finest!) Some of the other tracks were used in the Saturday morning cartoon "The Brady Kids." And in keeping with the Brady tradition of upstanding moral and social behavior, the "Kids From" album declares, "Save the Forests. This album is printed on recycled paper."

The fourth effort, "The Brady Bunch Phonographic Album," featured songs from the film *Tom Sawyer* (*not* the musicalized Johnnie Whitaker version) and the animated *Charlotte's Web*. As a promotional gig for the premiere of the latter, the Bradys performed "Zuckerman's Famous Pig" and "(Theme from) Charlotte's Web" at the Avco Theatre in Westwood Village, California, near the U.C.L.A. campus. These tickets were in such demand that when radio station KTAC announced it would award a ticket to the first 1,000 callers, the switchboard for the Tacoma/Seattle, Washington area broke down completely. The phone company requested that KTAC pull the spot off the air; an estimated 32,000 people had dialed the station's number at the same time.

The last of the Brady LPs, "Chris Knight and Maureen McCormick," seems a bit of a mismatch; the pairing was determined by the volume of fan mail each received. Unfortunately for Chris, his overwhelming popularity proved to be something of a burden. Not only did he believe he possessed absolutely no musical talent, he intensely disliked the album's cover and refused to promote it. Out of all the Brady albums, this one had the smallest release—and ranks among the rarest of Brady collectibles. All the leftover tracks were released as Maureen's singles, "Love's in the Roses,"/"Harmonize" and "Truckin' Back to You"/"Teeny Weeny Bit (Too Long)."

The last songs recorded by the Bunch were never committed to vinyl. Both tracks, "You've Got to Be in Love (to Love a Love Song)" and "Good Time Music," were recorded for the infamous episode #98, "Adios, Johnny Bravo," along with an ultra-distorted Greg solo number, "Heading To The Mountains." Also never released were Greg's try-out number, "Till There Was You," for the Banana Convention in episode #41, "Where There's Smoke," Florence and Maureen's Family Frolik Night's "Together Wherever We Go" from episode #81, "The Show Must

Go On??," and Robert and Barry's musicalized poetic reading of "The
Day Is Done" from the same episode.

Brady collectibles from the Fran and Michael Lerner collection — including (we are not making
this up) Brady Bunch cigar bands.

ALBUMS

"Merry Christmas from the Brady Bunch," Paramount #PAS 5026 November, 1971 (also on 8 track)

"Meet the Brady Bunch," Paramount #PAS 6032, 1972 (also on 8 track)

"The Kids from the Brady Bunch," Paramount #PAS 6037, 1972

"Phonographic Album," Paramount #PAS 6058, 1973

"Chris Knight and Maureen McCormick," Paramount #PAS 6062, 1973

(Florence Henderson) "Selections from Gypsy & Flower Drum Song," RCA Camden Records #CAL 560, 1959

(Florence Henderson) "With One More Look at You," Manhattan Records #MR LA 953H, 1979

SINGLES

"Frosty the Snowman"/"Silver Bells," Paramount #PAA 0062, 1970

"Time to Change"/"We Can Make the World a Whole Lot Brighter," Paramount #PAA 0141, 1972

"We'll Always Be Friends"/"Time To Change," Paramount #PAA 0167, 1972

"Candy Sugar Shop"/"Drummer Man," Paramount #PAA 180, 1972

"Zuckerman's Famous Pig"/"(Theme from) Charlotte's Web," Paramount #PAA 0205, 1973

"I'd Love You to Want Me"/"Everything I Do," Paramount #PAA 0229, 1973

SOLO SINGLES

Barry Williams: "Sweet Sweetheart"/"Sunny," Paramount #PAA 0122, 1970

Chris Knight: "Over And Over"/"Good For Each Other," Paramount #PAA 0177, 1972

Maureen McCormick: "Truckin' Back to You"/"Teeny Weeny Bit," Paramount #PAA 217, 1972

Maureen McCormick: "Little Bird"/"Just A-Singin' Alone," Paramount #PAA 0246, 1973

Maureen McCormick: "Love's In The Roses"/"Harmonize," Paramount #PAA 0292, 1973

Eve Plumb: "The Fortune Cookie Song"/"How Will It Be," RCA #0409, 1970

Mike Lookinland: "Love Doesn't Care Who's in It"/"Gum Drop," Capitol #CAP 3914, 1974

Florence Henderson: "Born to Say Goodbye"/"Can I Rely On You," ABC Records #12274, 1976

UNRELEASED SONGS PERFORMED ON "THE BRADY BUNCH"

"The Brady Bunch Theme Song" sung by The Peppermint Trolley Company (first season)

"O Come All Ye Faithful" — Episode #15

"Till There Was You" — Episode #41

"We Can Make the World a Whole Lot Brighter," guitar version — Episode #64

"Together Wherever We Go" — Episode #81

"The Day Is Done" (musicalized poetry reading) — Episode #81

"You've Got to Be in Love (to Love a Love Song)" — Episode #98

"Heading to the Mountains" — Episode #98

"Good Time Music" — Episode #98

SONGS RECORDED FOR BARRY WILLIAMS'S INCOMPLETE LP FOR PARAMOUNT

(Recorded between 9/24/71 and 3/23/72.)

"Sweet Sweetheart," "Early Days," "It Ought To Be Raining," "All She Wants To Be," "Cheyenne," "Sunny"

(*Note:* In 1978 Barry Williams recorded three songs with producer Mike Post, none of which were committed to vinyl.)

PAPERBACK BOOKS

(Published by Lancer Books, written by William Johnston, 1969-1970:)
The Brady Bunch

The Brady Bunch #2: Showdown At The P.T.A. Corral

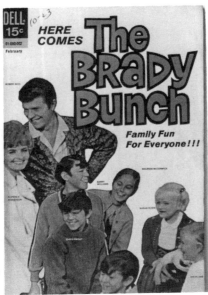

Family fun for everyone except Mike Lookinland, whose name does not appear above.

The Brady Bunch #3: Count Up To Blast-Down!

The Brady Bunch #4: The Bumbler Strikes Again

The Brady Bunch #5: The Quarterback Who Came To Dinner

(Published by Tigerbeat, written by Jack Matcha, 1972:)

The Brady Bunch: The Treasure of Mystery Island

The Brady Bunch in The New York Mystery

The Brady Bunch in Adventure On The High Seas

OTHER BOOKS

The Brady Bunch: Here Comes The Brady Bunch, Dell Publishing, February 1970, issue #1 (comic book)

The Brady Bunch: Why Parents Get Gray, Or 3 + 3 = Too Much!, Dell Publishing, May 1970, issue #2 (comic book)

The Brainy Bunch, Dell, 1970 (earliest known parody of the show)

The Brady Bunch Coloring Book (4 versions), Whitman, 1972, 73, 74 (2)

The Brady Bunch Activity Book, Whitman, 1974

The Brady Bunch Fun Kite Book, P.G.E., 1976 (comic book)

GAMES, TOYS, AND OTHER COLLECTIBLES

Kitty Karry-All Doll, Remco, 1969

Gum Cards (test set) 55 cards, Topps Chewing Gum, 1970

Gum Card Set 88 Cards, Topps Chewing Gum, 1971

Lunchbox & Thermos, King Sealy, 1970

"The Brady Bunch Grand
   Canyon Adventure"
   View-Master pack, GAF,
   1971

Talking View-Master Gift Pack
   II, GAF, 1971

The Brady Bunch Fan Club Kit,
   Tiger Beat, 1972

The Brady Bunch Frame Tray
   Puzzle, Whitman, 1972

Halloween Costume (Greg,
   Marcia), Collegeville, 1972

The Brady Bunch Paper Dolls
   (boxed, 3 sets), Whitman,
   1972-74

The Brady Bunch Paper Dolls
   (folder, 2 sets), Whitman,
   1973

"(I'm a) Yo-Yo Man" Sheet
   Music, Martin Cooper
   Music, 1973

The Brady Bunch Game,
   Whitman, 1973

The Brady Bunch Chess &
   Checkers, Larami, 1973

"The Grand Canyon Adventure" is the subject of three View-Master reels.

Greg and Marcia get down to their skivvies at last.

The Brady Bunch Banjo & Guitar, Larami, 1973

The Brady Bunch Hand Tambourine, Larami, 1973

The Brady Bunch Fishin' Fun Set, Larami, 1973

The Brady Bunch Supermarket (plastic grocery set), Larami, 1973

"I Saw The Brady Kids Live in Concert" 8x10 color picture, Pitts, 1973

"The Brady Kids" bracelet, Pitts, 1973

The Brady Bunch Outdoor Fun Playsets (4 sets), Larami, 1973 (slide,
   swing, gazebo, merry-go-round; each sold separately)

The Brady Bunch Hex-A-Game, Larami, 1973

The Brady Bunch Sticker Fun Book, Larami, 1973

The Brady Bunch Magic Slate, Larami, 1973

The Brady Bunch Toy Tea Set, Larami, 1973

The Brady Bunch 5 Tricky Puzzles, Larami, 1973

The Brady Bunch Dominoes, Larami, 1973

The Brady Bunch Purse, Larami, 1973

The Brady Bunch Jump Rope, Larami, 1973

Serving Tray, 1973 (Made for Sherwood Schwartz to hand out as Christmas gifts for the cast and crew)

Cigar Bands (unlicensed, set of 12), foreign, 1970s

OTHER BRADY-RELATED COLLECTIBLES

Music

"Home for the Holidays," MCA, 1978 (Christmas compilation including The Brady Bunch's "Jingle Bells")

"Weird Al Yankovic in 3D", Scotti Brothers Records, 1984 (Including "The Brady Bunch" theme sung to the tune of "The Safety Dance" by Men Without Hats)

"Lovedolls Superstars," We Got Power Films, 1984. "Sunshine Day," a rendition of the classic Brady version.

"Flipside Vinyl Fanzine Volume 1," Gafatanka, 1984. "We Three Bunch," sung by Adrenaline O.D.

"Television's Greatest Hits, Volume II," Tee Vee Toons, Inc., 1986 (Including "The Brady Bunch" theme song sung by the Brady Kids)

"Rerun Rock Presents Superstars Sing Television Themes", Rhino Records, Inc., 1989 (Scott Shaw sings "The Brady Bunch" theme song in the style of James Brown)

"Jan Brady" by the Lunachicks, (single) Blast First, 1989. A tribute from their EP "Sugar Luv."

"Butterfly Cove" by Steel Pole Bathtub, Boner Records, 1989 (Marcia's on the cover of this Bradyized punk album)

"They Drive Me Brady" (radio play), sung to the tune of "She Drives Me Crazy" by Fine Young Cannibals. Written and produced by Mark Davis and Rob "Iceman" Izenberg, 1990, the song came in #4 on Dr. Demento's syndicated radio show countdown for the year 1990.

"The Horny Bunch" (radio play) sung to the tune of "The Brady Bunch" theme song, written and produced by Davis/Izenberg, 1992.

"A TV Family Christmas," (CD & Cassette) Scotti Bros., 1992 (Christmas compilation including The Brady Bunch's "Rudolph the Red-Nosed Reindeer")

"Yesterday's Heroes: 70's Teen Idols," (CD) Rhino, 1992 (compilation including The Brady Bunch's "It's a Sunshine Day")

"Envy" by Eve's Plumb (Picture disc of Jan Brady) unlicensed, 1992

"It's A Sunshine Day—The Best of The Brady Bunch" (CD and cassette), MCA Records, Inc., 1993

"Jan's Theme (The Brady Bunch Song)" by Juicemaster (CD and cassette single), Cheese Factory Records, 1993

"TV Themes, Vol. 1," (Cassette) Sound Choices, 1993

Books

TV Guide cover, April 10, 1970

Dynamite magazine cover, Vol. 1, No. 2, Issue #39, August 1977, Scholastic Magazine

Dynamite magazine cover, Vol. 4, No. 2, Issue #75, August 1980, Scholastic Magazine

A Little Cooking, A Little Talking and a Whole Lot of Fun by Florence Henderson, JKF Marketing, 1984 (Robert Reed and Barry Williams are featured)

The Brady Bunch Book by Andy Edelstein and Frank Lovece. Warner Books, Inc., 1990

Growing Up Brady by Barry Williams with Chris Kreski. HarperCollins Publishers, Inc., 1992 (Foreword by Robert Reed)

Growing Up Brady narrated by Barry Williams (audio version), The Publishing Mills, 1992

Ann B. Davis: Alice's Brady Bunch Cookbook by Ann B. Davis, Ron Newcomer and Diane Smolen, Rutledge Hill Press, 1994

Videotapes
"A Very Brady Christmas," Paramount, 1992

Columbia House Videos, each featuring 4 uncut episodes. 1993-1994
"Bradys One & All, Vol. 1" (Comes with a Brady Bunch 25th anniversary pin)

"Brady vs. Brady, Vol. 2"

"The Littlest Brady, Vol. 3"

"Marcia Brady, Vol. 4"

"Greg Brady, Vol. 5"

"Brady in the Middle, Vol. 6"

"Bradys Run Amok, Vol. 7"

"Brady Lost & Found, Vol. 8"

"Battle of the Bradys, Vol. 9"

"Bradys under Par, Vol. 10"

Other
"The Brady Bunch" T-Shirts, Stanley DeSantis, 1993 (11 different styles including the girls, boys, Carol, Alice and "The Brady Bunch" theme song)

"The Brady Bunch" Wall Poster, OSP, 1993

THE BRADY KIDS, LIVE IN CONCERT!

Susan Olsen: "We all got keys to Atlanta. I'm wondering what this will do for me now. If I go to Atlanta now, can I go into the bars for free, or what?"

Joe Seiter (tour producer): "I was the seventh voice. I sang for Chris Knight, but I never told him. He was always live, but if everyone else's microphone was at 9, his would be at 2! And he would sing his little heart out!"

The Brady Kids hit the road.

The Brady albums, while not chartbusters, proved to be a modest financial success, and that's where the idea for the tour act came in. "It was kind of a joint decision between all the parents and me because I was the only one representing my own affairs," continues Barry. "Eve Plumb's father was in the music business, and

199

we hired a couple of Vegas producers, Joe Seiter and Ray Reese, who created an act for us. It was cute as heck."

"We came down to the studio, met the kids, and from there created, produced, choreographed, and staged the show. We even designed the costumes," says Joe Seiter. "We rehearsed all the time, five days a week." Rehearsals were held either in what is now Paramount's gym (at the time it was a dance space

Joe Seiter leads the bunch in rehearsals.

with bars and mirrors) or at Moro Landis Studios in Hollywood.

A proven jack-of-all-trades, Seiter also staged and choreographed the live Osmond Brothers shows. As a writer, he won two Emmys for his work on "The Andy Williams Show" and Shari Lewis' special, "A Picture of Us." As an announcer, he could be heard on such game shows as "You Don't Say," "The Liars Club" and "The Neighbors." He also has created a few game shows of his own, including CBS's "Give and Take." Today, he teaches computer science at a Los Angeles private school.

The Brady kids made their musical debut on the AGVA (Associated Guild Variety Artists)

With the sketches of their touring costumes.

awards, hosted by Ed Sullivan at Caesar's Palace, Las Vegas. They sang "Time To Change," choreographed by Jaime Rogers.

Their first gig under Seiter's direction began in February of 1972 at San Bernardino's Orange Show. Remembers Seiter, "Dick Clark was the promoter and he really liked us. The Barkays were also there. We did a 50's rock 'n' roll medley, and opened with 'Proud Mary.' It really cooked."

With a few minor changes, the Bradys set out on a multi-city tour. First stop: Savannah, Georgia, where they performed at the Civic Center Auditorium to a crowd of 7,500 on Friday, May 11, 1973. From there they traveled all over the South and as far north as Philadelphia. The following summer they toured the Pacific Northwest, with other appearances all around the country. Locally they performed at the Hollywood Bowl, Knott's Berry Farm, and on Dick Clark's American Bandstand. Their opening acts ranged from local jugglers to H.R. Pufnstuf to Tony Orlando and Dawn.

The arrangements were sent out to each city on the tour, and local musicians were hired for each performance. "We had a big orchestra," says Seiter, "not just a rock 'n' roll band. The arrangements weighed a ton. When we rehearsed down here we had real good guys who could read the charts, but everywhere we went it was a different story. We played in a little rodeo type place in Chahalis, Washington, and the band up there was awful. And what I thought was really stupid was that about two hundred yards from the stage was a railroad. The trains came through at least three times during the show. You couldn't hear a thing, but the audience loved us, and it was the best show we did up there! Go figure."

Live, from Chahalis, Washington—it's the Brady Kids, backed by a freight train!

Finding a good pick-up band wasn't the only problem that plagued the Bradys. "Wherever we'd go we'd have some kind of problem," says Seiter. "I remember walking into a place in Knoxville, Tennessee, and this guy said, 'What can I do for you?', and I said, 'Well, it's eleven and we have a show at two and we'd like to get in and set up.' And he said, 'Is that today? Well, I better go get Clem and have him open up for you all then.' No posters were set up, they were all in the back office. But we did pretty good business."

Says Susan Olsen, "There were riots. Fans got out of hand. They tipped over a VW van because they thought it was the boys' dressing room. I think it was in Savannah. There was one town where they let school out for the day because the Brady kids were in town. It was like we were Elvis, and we would have to sneak out and run through tunnels to get out to these cars. Then the drivers would drive like maniacs to ditch the cars that would be following to get us to the hotel so nobody would know where we were staying. The whole thing was so silly."

After a couple of bad experiences at department stores, record sign-

The Minnesota State Fair: The Kids beat a hasty retreat.

ings were canceled due to crowd control problems. And in Philadelphia, the Mike Douglas Show staff didn't even know they were scheduled until they arrived! Says Susan, "We did the 'Mike Douglas Show' with Liberace, and we did the limbo with him. He loved us so much that he wanted to take us on tour with him. We were pretty uncool, but that was *really* uncool!"

There's always that solo career to fall back on.

When fashions were simpler.

BRADY TV SPINOFFS

In cartoons, the stars can't grow up.

THE BRADY KIDS

Concurrent with "The Brady Bunch," this animated Saturday morning show focused on the Brady kids' school lives and everyday adolescent problems, sans parental interference. Tiger is traded in for Mop Top, the talking dog. Added to the menagerie are Marlon the magical mynah bird, whose talents include ventriloquism and impersonations, and Ping and Pong, two panda bears who only speak Chinese. Instead of cohabitating in Mike's Danish-modern spread, they live in a treehouse, where they form a successful rock band. Too much fun!

Filmation's Lou Scheimer and Norm Prescott, who also animated "Gilligan's Planet" and "The New Adventures of Gilligan," headed the project. Recalls Sherwood, "I had a less active hand in it, but it taught me a lesson. I wanted that show to be very imaginative, that was my agreement with Lou and Norm. But it was not satisfactory as far as I was concerned because they got into school problems and things I didn't want. I wanted it to be the kids' imagination let loose. And it taught me that I just couldn't let it go. I would have to read and critique each script in order to get what I wanted, and I did that with the other two Gilligan projects."

Despite these misgivings, twenty-two episodes were made, which aired over two seasons.

THE BRADY KIDS

22 half-hours on ABC
Saturdays 10:30-11:00 am (season 1)
Saturdays 11:00-11:30 am (season 2)

EXECUTIVE PRODUCER:	Sherwood Schwartz
PRODUCERS:	Lou Scheimer and Norm Prescott, Filmation Associates
WRITER:	Marc Richards
DIRECTOR:	Hal Sutherland
MUSIC:	Yvetta Blais and Jeff Michaels
FIRST TELECAST:	September 9, 1972
LAST TELECAST:	August 31, 1974
CAST:	Greg Brady . . . . Barry Williams
	Peter Brady . . . . Christopher Knight
	Bobby Brady . . . . Mike Lookinland
	Marcia Brady . . . . Maureen McCormick
	Jan Brady . . . . Eve Plumb
	Cindy Brady . . . . Susan Olsen
	Mop Top . . . . Larry Storch
	Marlon . . . . Larry Storch
	Ping and Pong . . . . Jane Webb

❀   ❀   ❀

THE BRADY BUNCH VARIETY HOUR

"I had nothing to do with it. Zip. Sid and Marty Krofft did it and they had to pay for it later," remarks an annoyed Sherwood Schwartz. Apparently, Fred Silverman, president of ABC at the time, caught Florence Henderson and some of the Brady kids on the Kroffts' show, "Donny & Marie," and approached them with a similar concept involving the Bradys. Without Sherwood and Paramount's knowledge or permission, they went ahead with it, and on November 28, 1976, "The Brady Bunch

Play that funky music.

Variety Hour" debuted. Except for Eve Plumb, who was replaced by Geri Reischl, all the Bradys participated, performing a number of mediocre comedy/musical variety acts, complete with swimming pool. Says Sherwood, "I discussed this with Paramount, and we could have put a stop to it, but there were two pluses. One is that if they're on the air every week then that, in effect, is promoting the Brady family again. Secondly, they have to pay a royalty to Paramount and to me. So we let them do it."

"The Brady Bunch Variety Hour" served as the pilot for the upcoming "Brady Bunch Hour." Fasten your seatbelts; eight more of these gems followed! It's worth noting that this initial variety special was selected by the Nickelodeon network as the crowning midnight broadcast on a recent New Year's Eve high-camp rerun marathon.

THE BRADY BUNCH VARIETY HOUR
Sunday, November 28, 1976 on ABC
7:00-8:00pm

EXECUTIVE
PRODUCERS: Sid and Marty Krofft
PRODUCERS: Lee Miller and Jerry McPhie
WRITERS: Carl Kleinschmitt, Ronny Graham, Terry Hart,
Bruce Vilanch, Steve Bluestein
DIRECTOR: Art Fisher
FEATURING: The Kroffette Dancers and the Water Follies
Swimmers
CAST: Mike Brady . . . . Robert Reed
Carol Brady . . . . Florence Henderson
Greg Brady . . . . Barry Williams
Peter Brady . . . . Christopher Knight
Bobby Brady . . . . Mike Lookinland
Marcia Brady . . . . Maureen McCormick
Jan Brady . . . . Geri Reischl
Cindy Brady . . . . Susan Olsen
Alice . . . . Ann B. Davis
Guests: . . . . Tony Randall,
Donny and Marie
Osmond

SONGS: "Baby Face" (Bradys)
"One" (Bradys)
"Everything Has Its Season" (Barry)
"What I Did For Love" (Florence)
"Memories" (Florence)
"The Way We Were" (Florence)
"I'm In Heaven" (Florence and Robert Reed)
"Dance With Me" (Bradys)
"I Could Have Danced All Night" (Florence)
"The Hustle" (Bradys)
"Shake Your Bootie" (Bradys and Ann B. Davis)

✿   ✿   ✿

THE BRADY BUNCH HOUR

> "I did it because I didn't have anything better to do.
> I was going to school and I really wanted to work.
> It was fun. But it was also really embarrassing."
> — Susan Olsen

"The Brady Bunch Hour" was originally scheduled to air every fifth week in the "Nancy Drew/Hardy Boys Mysteries" time slot on Sundays at 7:00pm on ABC. However, the show bounced around in various time slots and days, making it a challenge for any Brady fan to find.

All the Bradys returned except for Eve Plumb, who was replaced by Geri Reischl. Mike gives up his career as an architect to manage the family's variety show. And—watch out—the Bradys trade in their suburban house for a new beachfront home! And a one, and a two. . .

THE BRADY BUNCH HOUR
8 one hour shows on ABC, various nights and times.

Do you get the feeling Robert Reed doesn't like his tie?

EXECUTIVE
PRODUCERS: Sid and Marty Krofft
PRODUCER: Lee Miller
CO-PRODUCER: Tom Swale
WRITERS: Ronny Graham, Bruce Vilanch, Steve Bluestein, Mike Kagan and Carl Kleinschmitt
DIRECTOR: Jack Regas
MUSICAL
DIRECTOR: George Wyle
MUSICAL
ARRANGEMENTS: Sid Feller, Van Alexander
CHOREOGRAPHER: Joe Cassini
COSTUME
DESIGNER: Peter Menefee
FIRST TELECAST: January 23, 1977
LAST TELECAST: May 25, 1977
CAST: Mike Brady . . . . Robert Reed
Carol Brady . . . . Florence Henderson
Greg Brady . . . . Barry Williams
Peter Brady . . . . Christopher Knight
Bobby Brady . . . . Mike Lookinland
Marcia Brady . . . . Maureen McCormick
Jan Brady . . . . Geri Reischl
Cindy Brady . . . . Susan Olsen
Alice Nelson . . . . Ann B. Davis
REGULARS: Rip Taylor as Merrill, The Krofftette Dancers, The Water Follies Swimmers

THE BRADY GIRLS GET MARRIED: "THE BRADY BRIDES"

Originally, "The Brady Girls Get Married" was produced as a two-hour TV movie for NBC to be aired on February 6, 1981, 8:00-10:00 pm. (This despite a full-page ad in TV Guide proclaiming it as a *ninety-minute* movie, airing 8:30-10:00 pm.) However, at the last minute, Fred Silverman, NBC's former president, decided to pull it. Remembers Sherwood,

"He asked me to chop it into four pieces. Then he would add six more and we would have ten shows to give it a shot as a series. We had to recut the whole show. As a producer, you *design* a show, and Lloyd and I designed a two-hour show with an overall story. You can't chop it into half-hour pieces suddenly, but that's what we had to do." Beginning with the fourth episode, the title was changed to "The Brady Brides."

Although further episodes weren't ordered, the show did garner positive reviews. *Variety* , which had crucified "The Brady Bunch" in the past, said, "It's all executed smoothly, the teleplay by

Good reviews for a change: the smiling regulars from "The Brady Brides."

Sherwood and Lloyd Schwartz, who also created the project, is a good one. The transition from kids to grownups comes off well, and the humor flows naturally and easily." Reflects Sherwood, "It was fairly successful at the time, when NBC had nothing more successful to put on the air."

Later that year, the first four episodes were edited back into its original two-hour movie format titled, "The Brady Girls Get Married," which aired on Tuesday, October 27, 1981 from 9:00-11:00 pm on NBC.

THE BRADY BRIDES
10 half hour shows on NBC
Fridays 8:30-9:00 pm

EXECUTIVE
PRODUCERS: Sherwood Schwartz and Lloyd J. Schwartz
PRODUCER: John Thomas Lenox
ASSOCIATE
PRODUCER: Samuel Vance
WRITERS: Sherwood Schwartz, Lloyd J. Schwartz, Warren

Murray, Philip John Taylor, Mara Lideks, Hope
Sherwood, Mark Esslinger, Richard Gurman
DIRECTORS: Peter Baldwin, Alan Myerson, Herbert Kenwith,
Tony Mordente
MUSIC: Frank DeVol
FIRST TELECAST: February 6, 1981
LAST TELECAST: April 17, 1981
CAST: Marcia Brady Logan . . . . . . Maureen McCormick
Jan Brady Covington. . . . . . Eve Plumb
Wally Logan . . . . Jerry Houser
Philip Covington III. . . . . . . Ron Kuhlman
Ann Nelson Franklin . . . . . . Ann B. Davis
Carol Brady . . . . Florence Henderson
Harry (episode #5). . . . . Keland Love

A VERY BRADY CHRISTMAS

> Sherwood Schwartz: "As the men arrived, one af-
> ter the other, they showed up with moustaches. All
> of them! Bob, Barry, Chris, and Mike. And I said,
> 'Now wait a minute, we can't have this. Two of you
> are going to have to shave it off, or else it will turn
> into A Very Brady Moustache!'"

Debuting on Sunday, December 18, 1988, "A Very Brady Christmas" was CBS's highest-rated TV movie of that year too. Following its
premiere broadcast, the telepicture elevated CBS's third-place ranking to
the number-two spot for the first time that season in the weekly ratings
race. The Bradys also earned a footnote in television history by airing on
all three networks. (NBC had tried its hand in 1981 with "The Brady
Brides.") Quite impressive!

A lot has changed since we last saw the bunch back in '81. Greg has
married his nurse, Nora. Peter is a frustrated salesman who is in love with

On the set for "A Very Brady Christmas." That's Sherwood Schwartz in the middle.

his boss. Marcia and jobless Wally have two kids, Jessica and Mickey. Jan's marriage to Philip is on the rocks. Bobby dropped out of school (unbeknownst to the folks) to pursue his dream of becoming a race car driver, and Cindy is a senior at U of A, wherever that is. The entire Brady cast, as well as extended family, return, except for Susan Olsen, who was, in real life, off honeymooning with her new (and now former) husband, Steve Ventimiglia. Jennifer Runyon filled her shoes for this yuletide gathering. Alice also lands on their doorstep after Sam leaves her for a younger chicken.

Mike and Carol use the money from their vacation account to bring the family together for a Christmas reunion. Most of the story revolves around everyone coming in from all over the country and Carol figuring out who's going to sleep where, and with whom, in their newly modernized home. In case you missed it, the family room is now an exercise room, and a *new room* was introduced: a bathroom to the right of the

main staircase. As if that
weren't enough, the door at
the top of the staircase is
open! A first in Brady history. We don't actually get to
see *inside* these mystery
rooms, of course.

The story ends when
Mike has to leave Christmas
dinner to check out a problem at a construction site. He
gets trapped when a section
of the building collapses, but
pulls through in the end.
(After all, this is a Christmas
film.) Recapping the good
old days, all gather around to
sing, "O Come, All Ye Faithful."

Mike Lookinland and Christopher Knight relax between
takes of "A Very Brady Christmas."

Says Sherwood, "The success of it was a combination of two things.
One was the fact that it was Christmas time, which is family time, so it
was a perfect opportunity to bring them back. And number two, many
people wanted to know what they looked like. There was a great longing
to see what happens. It's like with any family reunion."

A VERY BRADY CHRISTMAS
Sunday, December 18, 1988 on CBS, 9:00-11:00 pm

EXECUTIVE
PRODUCER: Sherwood Schwartz
PRODUCERS: Lloyd Schwartz and Barry Berg
WRITERS: Sherwood and Lloyd Schwartz
DIRECTOR: Peter Baldwin
MUSIC: Laurence Juber
CAST: Mike Brady . . . . Robert Reed
Carol Brady . . . . Florence Henderson
Alice Nelson Franklin . . . . . Ann B. Davis

Greg Brady . . . . Barry Williams
Peter Brady . . . . Christopher Knight
Bobby Brady . . . . Mike Lookinland
Marcia Brady Logan . . . . . . Maureen McCormick
Jan Brady Covington. . . . . . Eve Plumb
Cindy Brady . . . . Jennifer Runyon
Nora Brady . . . . Caryn Richman
Valerie Thomas . . . . Carol Huston
Wally Logan . . . . Jerry Houser
Philip Covington III. . . . . . . Ron Kuhlman
Jessica Logan. . . . . Jaclyn Bernstein
Mickey Logan . . . . G.W. Lee
Kevin Brady . . . . Zachary Bostrom
Leonard Prescott . . . . F.J. O'Neil
Mrs. Powell . . . . Barbara Mallory
Mr. Powell . . . . Nick Toth
Ms. Crane . . . . Selma Archerd
Belinda. . . . . Tonya Lee Williams
TV announcer . . . . Ines Pedroza
Sam Franklin . . . . Lewis Arquette
Howie . . . . Lenny Garner
Donald . . . . Doug Carfrae
Amy. . . . . Frances Louise Turner
police chief . . . . Gerry Black
receptionist. . . . . Patricia Mullins
guard #1 . . . . Jack Kutcher
guard #2 . . . . Gilbert G. Garcia
mechanic . . . . Bart Braverman
Ted Roberts . . . . Phillip Richard Allen

❀   ❀   ❀

THE BRADYS

Barry Williams: "Greg being an ObGYN was perfect. That I was married to Gidget was good, and that I had kind of a nerdy son was good, too."

Martha Quinn: "They told me I was getting my own square, but I shouldn't be too excited because it was small. I said, I don't care how big it is, I'm in a Brady square!"

As with the NBC "Brady Brides" deal, CBS originally ordered two two-hour TV movies from Sherwood and son Lloyd. "The shows were specifically designed for the May and November sweeps," remembers Sherwood. "The May

Filming "The Bradys."

sweeps prompted us to do a racetrack story, taking advantage of the publicity the Indianapolis 500 would be getting. And then we had planned an election script to be aired the first week of November. Suddenly, CBS was in need of a series. They were desperate, so it seemed logical at the time."

Six hour-long episodes were produced as a mid-season replacement. And on Friday, February 9, 1990, "The Bradys" made its comeback in the 8:00 pm time slot. Everyone returned except for Maureen McCormick, who was replaced by Leah Ayres ("First And Ten," "St. Elsewhere," "Edge of Night"). Says Sherwood, "I begged CBS to put it at 9:00 pm because the people who wanted to see it are in their twenties and thirties—they're not kids anymore. They can't relate to 8:00 pm. The story lines are more appropriate for an older audience. But they didn't listen."

Fondly referred to as "Bradysomething" by its cast and crew, this dramedy brings the Bradys face to face with nineties kinds of problems such as infertility, unemployment, alcoholism, and paralysis. Gone are the good old days when getting braces, being afraid of high school, and singing in the Glee Club were monumental problems!

Mike wins the City Council seat.

Although the first two-hour movie pilot fared moderately well, the following four episodes dropped into the bottom twenty of the Nielsen ratings and stayed there. "People weren't interested in the extended families," reflects Sherwood. Expanding on this, Barry says, "There were too many people. I think there's a nostalgic interest in our show, not a contemporary interest in who we are now. You can do it as a one-shot and it's fun and people can tune in for a couple hours and check it out, but not to develop a new legion of fans."

If "The Bradys" had been a success, however, Sherwood had plans to kill off the family's patriarch, Mike Brady! (A similar line of thought had emerged at Paramount at the conclusion of the original series' fifth season.) "We were going to have Mike accidentally killed in a helicopter crash. As a City Councilman, he was going to check out a fire to see if the fire department needed more backroads, and the helicopter [would go down]. Bob [Robert Reed] didn't know about this. I was fed up with him. The story would go on with the kids trying to fix up their mother."

To date, this marks the last of the Brady revival attempts, and according to Sherwood, nothing is in the works.

THE BRADYS

1 two-hour show, 4 one hour shows on CBS
Fridays 8:00-10:00 pm, 8:00-9:00 pm.

EXECUTIVE PRODUCER:	Sherwood Schwartz	
CO-EXECUTIVE PRODUCER:	Lloyd J. Schwartz	
PRODUCER:	Barry Berg	
WRITERS:	Sherwood Schwartz, Lloyd J. Schwartz, Sandra Kay Siegel, Ed Scharlach	
DIRECTORS:	Bruce Bilson, Bob Sweeney, Nancy Malone, Dick Martin	
MUSIC:	Laurence Juber	
FIRST TELECAST:	(Movie pilot) Friday, February 9, 1990 8:00-10:00 pm	
LAST TELECAST:	Friday, March 2, 1990 8:00-9:00 pm	
CAST:	Mike Brady	Robert Reed
	Carol Brady	Florence Henderson
	Greg Brady	Barry Williams
	Peter Brady	Christopher Knight
	Bobby Brady	Mike Lookinland
	Marcia Brady Logan	Leah Ayres
	Jan Brady Covington	Eve Plumb
	Cindy Brady	Susan Olsen
	Alice Nelson Franklin	Ann B. Davis
	Wally Logan	Jerry Houser
	Philip Covington III.	Ron Kuhlman
	Gary Greenberg	Ken Michelman
	Nora Brady	Caryn Richman
	Tracy Wagner Brady	Martha Quinn
	Mickey Logan	Michael Melby
	Jessica Logan.	Jaclyn Bernstein
	Kevin Brady	Jonathan Weiss
	Patti Covington	Valerie Ick

THE BRADY LEGEND LIVES ON

> Jill Soloway, producer (to the L.A. *Daily News*): "I think everybody had this weird sort of feeling of Marcia and Greg being almost a secret couple. You were always wondering, 'Is the day ever going to come when they're going to kiss or something?' It never did, but if you watch the episodes closely, they flirt with each other a lot."
>
> Becky Thyre (on playing Marcia on *The Real Live Brady Bunch*): "She's always bitchy and pouty and she tries to be sexy all the time. When she's standing in a room she doesn't just stand there, she poses!"
>
> Melanie Hutsell (on playing Jan on *The Real Live Brady Bunch*): "Jan kinda always looks constipated. She always has such an intense look on her face, and she's real breathy in the way she speaks."

"The Brady Bunch" has probably received more tribute than any other program in TV history. Although the most recent incarnation, "The Bradys," proved unsuccessful, the thirst for more has not been quenched. "The Brady Bunch" has become the touchstone of a whole generation, thriving in conversation, comic strips, greeting cards, television, movies, theatre and books. Here are a few recent examples.

The stage show *The Real Live Brady Bunch* got its start when a friend of producer-sisters Faith and Jill Soloway performed her dead-on imitation of Jan Brady. Intrigued by the possibilities, the sisters began to tape and transcribed each episode for performance by Chicago's Annoyance Theatre troupe. When Sherwood saw the stage show, he recommended to Paramount that the group pay only a token sum to acknowledge the copyright. From that point on, the sisters had access to the original teleplays.

The show made its debut on June 19, 1990. The featured episode was performed deadpan, the script recounted verbatim by adults portraying their juvenile counterparts. The stage was bare, the props minimal, and the 110-seat theatre rustic at best. If you were lucky, you sat in a folding chair; otherwise you had a space on the carpeted floor. The Soloways' friend Becky Thyre, by the way, ended up being cast as Marcia, to whom she bears an eerie resemblance. She performs Marcia's hair flip and sashay with remarkable accuracy.

The sisters doubted the show would generate much interest. If anything, it amused the two

The cast of "The Real Live Brady Bunch."

A shot from the Los Angeles premier ("The Subject Was Noses").

of them. But word got out, lines formed around the block, and the $7 tickets were soon the hottest in town. The audiences tended to be homogeneous, a group of men and women ranging from their early twenties to their early thirties. For many it was a chance to relive days gone by, to be once more an intimate part of the family they wanted, and had always wanted, to belong to.

In a style reminiscent of *The Rocky Horror Picture Show*, the show often prompted outbursts, with the audience passionately reciting the dialogue along with the cast. Upon hearing the opening chords of the theme song, they'd enthusiastically sing along as the cast formed the tic-tac-toe grid on stage. It was surreal, it was simple. It worked. The show was a huge hit.

It didn't take long for the media to catch on, and soon the production won national attention. Many original Bradys came to check it out, and Eve Plumb even made an appearance as Tami Cutler, Greg's agent, in the episode, "Adios, Johnny Bravo" (#98). It was a dream come true for the Soloway sisters. Sherwood Schwartz also witnessed the phenomenon and was introduced at the end of the show. "I had to go up on stage and answer a lot of trivia questions, and they wouldn't stop screaming. They kept shouting, Sher-wood, Sherwood. It was the most incredible experience I ever had."

Deja vu all over again. That's Eve Plumb (who played Jan in the series) at far right in the role of Tami Cutler in the stage recreation of "Adios, Johnny Bravo."

The show was on a roll. Eventually it caught the eye of New York producer-promoter Ron Delsener, who brought it to the 375-seat Village Gate Theatre in New York. Passing the torch to a replacement cast in Chicago, the Annoyance troupe made its New York debut on September 19, 1991. The ticket price skyrocketed to $20-$25.

Concurrent with the New York production, the show made its Los Angeles debut on April 21, 1992, at the Westwood Playhouse, featuring the episode "The Subject Was Noses" (#90). Naturally, it sold out!

A year later the show went on the road for a 40-week, 45-city U.S. tour—for eight weeks of which Davy Jones graced the stage reprising his role in "Getting Davy Jones" (episode #63—see photo on page 55).

However, sadly enough, all good things must come to an end. On Sunday, May 8th, 1994, *The Real Live Brady Bunch* ended its run in Scottsdale, Arizona.

✿ ✿ ✿

Ross Harper (C.B. Barnes on "Day By Day"): "It's more than just a show, it's a way of life. Whenever I have a problem that's insurmountable, I turn to 'The Brady Bunch' for guidance."

The Bradys have been satirized on television countless times, most recently on "Saturday Night Live." In a hilarious skit featured on February 8, 1992, host Susan Dey reprises her role as Laurie Partridge, while the other SNL players fill in for the rest of the family. As they rehearse in their garage/studio, Jan Brady, played by Melanie Hutsell—the former Jan on *The Real Live Brady Bunch* and now a regular on SNL—drops in, followed by the rest of the "Bradys." Before you know it, they engage in a "Battle of the Bands." TV at its finest! (Incidentally, Andy Richter, who played Mike Brady for a year in *The Real Live Brady Bunch*, also landed on network television as talk show host Conan O'Brien's sidekick.)

An episode of Nickelodeon's sitcom "Hi Honey, I'm Home" brought Ann B. Davis back as Alice. The show revolves around the Nielsens, a fifties TV sitcom family who live in modern-day New Jersey, where they have been relocated by the Sitcom Relocation Program. The Nielsens await a chance to go back on TV, but in this particular episode they are in competition with the Bradys!

The funniest Brady spoof to date first aired on February 5, 1989 on NBC's "Day By Day." Teenager Ross Harper (C.B. Barnes) comes home with an F on a history paper. His homework, you see, conflicted with a "Brady Bunch" marathon: "You miss one and you lose the flow," he explains to his parents. Contrary to what Mike and Carol might do, Ross gets yelled at, but that doesn't stop him from watching more of the re-runs. He falls asleep and wakes up as Chuck Brady, the lost Brady sibling.

To his horror, Chuck/Ross discovers he's dressed in typical Brady garb: bell bottoms, polyester shirt, and platform shoes: "Does it concern you that I'm wearing high heels?" he asks. When Mike tells him, "You have to do something about your hair," Chuck/Ross retorts that his hair is "sacred," and refuses cut it. Mike replies, "I don't want you to cut it. You have to get it permed. All the Brady men have perms."

The thrill of meeting "Mom" and "Dad," Peter, Bobby, Marcia (very pregnant), and Alice soon wears thin; Mike and Carol start repeating dialogue. After all, it's a rerun. Chuck/Ross wakes up, relieved to be back at the Harper house.

The show also featured references to a medley of original Brady episodes, including Buddy Hinton, the roaring twenties party, the Bears cheerleading chant, and the "Vote For Brady" episode—only this time it's Chuck/Ross who rivals Marcia for Student Body President.

It was one of "Day by Day's" highest-rated shows. True Brady fans, although they appreciated the laughs, did note one glaring discrepancy, however. On the set of this production there were only nine steps leading up to the second floor. On "The Brady Bunch," there were, of course, twelve.

✿   ✿   ✿

Brady Network, Brady Physics, and Brady Metaphysics. These were all categories featured on MTV's game show parody, "Remote Control," hosted by Ken Ober. The show has since been canceled, but not before bonafide Bradys Barry Williams, Eve Plumb, and Susan Olsen went head-to-head for charity on September 23, 1989.

Questions ranged from "How many times did Mike get Carol pregnant?" to "Which Brady did not appear on 'A Very Brady Christmas?'" Barry beat Susan to the buzzer on this one although it was Susan herself who was the no-show. But you knew that. Eventually Barry beat Eve, 115-90.

"THE BRADY BUNCH"

HOT MOVIE, COLD SHOULDER: MY STRUGGLE TO GET THE INSIDE SCOOP ON THE NEW BRADY BUNCH MOVIE

One would think that being the author of a book on the movie's subject, and a professional at a local TV station *just down the block* from Paramount Pictures, would get me on the set of the new Brady Bunch movie. I thought I was a shoo-in. I thought I'd get a one-liner, or a chance to be an extra. I thought I'd have the chance to hobnob with "Marcia" and "Jan"—and bring you the behind-the-scenes scoop. No way.

In a nutshell, I was blackballed.

At least one source involved with the production of the film was up front with me about the reason for the cold shoulder I received. The Powers That Be feared that I would disclose the film's Secret Plot, thereby ruining the fun for millions of Brady fans. The cast interviews I set up were all canceled. Phone calls went unreturned. Even my request for a press kit was denied. All because of studio paranoia that I would somehow compromise the project by leaking details of the story.

So—you want to hear about the plot of this movie?

But wait—I'm getting ahead of myself. I was itching to see *something*, and it just so happened that I was able to obtain the Bunch's shooting schedule. With

The fictional West Dale High

this in hand, I hopped into my car and cruised over to a local high school that had been turned into "West Dale High." There was no action in front, so I walked around the back, and, lo and behold, a scene for the film was being shot in a classroom! Before I could really check it out, though, an attack dog production assistant came after me, and I was unceremoniously escorted off the set. To add insult to injury, copies of the first edition of this book were all over the place. I counted three well-used, dog-eared copies around the set. Nevertheless, I was banished.

I put a call in to the production office at Paramount, but I could only reach the associate producer's voice mail. I left a message: "If I sign a statement guaranteeing that I will not disclose the Secret Plot, can I visit the set?" The result? You guessed it. No return call.

Now, as it turned out, the plot had *already* partially been leaked by two major Los Angeles newspapers whose combined circulations total over two million. Go figure. (Those pieces, by the way, were *reportedly* authorized by the film's director, Betty Thomas—who won a directing Emmy for *Dream On* and acted in *Hill Street Blues*.) So, with the power of Freedom of Speech on my side, here's the Secret Plot. If you don't want to know about it, skip the next paragraph!

The Bradys' neighbors, the Dittmeyers (played by Michael McKean and Jean Smart), who were never seen once in five seasons of the actual show, are central to this story. Mr. Dittmeyer is a real estate agent who gets the residents of the whole block to sell their homes to make room for a mall. Well, nearly all the residents. The Bradys don't sell. Things get goofy when the Bradys, who still live in the '70s, come up against the harsh reality of the '90s. Carol is played by Shelley (*Cheers*) Long; Mike is played by Gary (*Midnight Caller*) Cole. The roles of the children are filled by lesser-known actors cast largely for their resemblance to the originals. You might remember Chris Barnes, who plays Greg Brady, from the celebrated "Day by Day" episode in which his character dreamed he was a fourth Brady boy (see page 221).

As luck would have it, I was able to secure a short interview with James Berg and Stan Zimmerman, who will receive writing credit on the film along with Bonnie and Terry Turner, Laurence Elehwany and Rick Copp, and Sherwood and Lloyd Schwartz. Berg and Zimmerman, whose skill, insight, and intelligence were evident to me the moment they referred to this book as their "bible," are known primarily as the writers who wrote the "Roseanne" episode in which Roseanne smooches Mariel Hemingway! (As a matter of fact, Berg and Zimmerman wrote Roseanne into the Brady script as a disgruntled neighbor, but she declined the role.)

Speaking of alternative lifestyles, an early draft of the screenplay by Bonnie and Terry Turner had Marcia digging girls more than guys, Mike flipping burgers for a living, and Alice sleeping with door-to-door salesmen. This approach is perhaps what one would expect from two former *Saturday Night Live* writers; the Turners also scripted the successful *Wayne's World* movies. Of the Turner draft, Sherwood Schwartz said to the *Daily News*, "It was an assassination. It was just awful. They were using words that are not for family viewing." Numerous rewrites followed, and the Schwartzes are now satisfied with the current version.

For value-added appeal, all the surviving members of the original Brady cast were offered cameos in the picture; Florence Henderson, Maureen McCormick, Eve Plumb, and Christopher Knight declined. I guess Henderson is too busy doing those "Kurtain Kraft" infomercials. She was to have played a chain-smoking truck driver who supports her six grown children working long hours in the cab of an eighteen-wheeler. On her route, she would have picked up a runaway "Jan" and returned her safely home. Her CB handle was going to be—ready?—"Wessonality."

As Florence said to *Star* magazine, "I turned down the cameo because it wasn't funny. I couldn't find the humor in it. I just didn't get it. It was full of cheap humor. Why they would want to depict me or any of the others in such a degrading manner is just beyond me. At first, I thought they would have me play someone like 'Carol's' mom. Now that would have been fun." The rumor mill also has it that Henderson was only offered a measly $5,000 for her appearance. "I don't get out of bed for that kind of money," Henderson said of the offer. Apparently the other nonparticipants felt basically the same way.

So Henderson's role was rewritten for Ann B. Davis, who is, as of this writing, expected to appear in the film. Also keep an eye out for Barry "music producer" Williams, Mike "police officer" Lookinland, and Susan "reporter for the *National Tattler*" Olsen. Davy Jones will also repeat his role.

Rebuilding 4222 Clinton Way . . .

. . . but you'll have to see the movie to get a look at the finished product.

Because the facade of the original Brady house used for the exterior shots had changed drastically over the years, a substitute location had to be found. Not more than two miles away from the genuine article, in the San Fernando Valley, a false facade was built in front of an existing home, covering it completely. I was able to snap a couple of shots capturing the early stages of the change (the photos are featured here), but was, alas, unable to get a shot of the end result. The day I tried, a big dumpster was strategically placed in front of the house. When I made my way around the blockade, a big, beefy guard told me to "take a hike."

As I write this, it is uncertain when the Brady Bunch movie will be released. I've heard several dates; a good many phone calls placed to just about everyone at Paramount have gone unreturned. I think there is a pattern emerging here.

Do you suppose they'll invite me to the premiere?

THE BRADY BUNCH (Motion Picture)

PRODUCERS: Sherwood Schwartz, Lloyd Schwartz, Alan Ladd Jr.
CO-PRODUCERS: Barry Berg, Jenno Topping

DIRECTOR: Betty Thomas
SCREENPLAY: Sherwood Schwartz, Lloyd Schwartz, Laurice Elehwany, Rick Copp, Bonnie Turner, Terry Turner, James Berg, and Stan Zimmerman

CAST:		
Carol Brady	. . . .	Shelley Long
Mike Brady	. . . .	Gary Cole
Alice	. . . .	Henriette Mantel
Marcia Brady	. . . .	Christine Taylor
Jan Brady	. . . .	Jennifer Cox
Cindy Brady	. . . .	Olivia Hack
Greg Brady	. . . .	Christopher Barnes
Peter Brady	. . . .	Paul Sutera
Bobby Brady	. . . .	Jesse Lee
Mr. Dittmeyer	. . . .	Michael McKean
Mrs. Dittmeyer	. . . .	Jean Smart
Sam	. . . .	Dave Graf

A BRADY FAMILY ALBUM

Some never-before-published shots from behind the scenes

Mike Lookinland between scenes.

Robert Reed takes the kids and studio teacher Mrs. Whitfield—as well as his parents—on a tour on board the Queen Elizabeth II.

Sherwood Schwartz and Susan Olsen at a "Happy Hiatus" party thrown early in the show's run.

The kids blow out the candles on their "Happy Hiatus" cake.

HAPPY BIRTHDAY, MR. SCHWARTZ

~~THERE'S A BIRTHDAY OF A MAN WHO'S~~

~~THERE'S A BIRTHDAY OF A MAN WHO'S SPECIAL~~

~~WHO IS SPECIALLY~~

There's a birthday of a man who's special –
Who is specially loved by all the Brady Bunch –
He's the kindest guy around and the sharpest –
We know – that's not a hunch!

It's the birthday of a man named Sherwood
Who can see the forest as he sees the trees –
And we wish him/all the best   forever
But not a life of ease –

For we'd like him to keep ~~making~~ THINKING up good stories
For the Brady Bunch to play in on T.V
And we wish him now the happiest of birthdays
And hope there'll always be
THE BRADY BUNCH, THE BRADY BUNCH –
That's the way we can stay THE BRADY BUNCH!

Susan Olsen, Mike Lookinland, and tour producer Joe Seiter go looking for shoes.

A poem, set to the tune of the Brady Bunch theme, that the kids wrote in honor of Sherwood's birthday.

Christopher Knight, Eve Plumb, and Mike Lookinland relax in Hawaii.

Mike Lookinland and Christopher Knight between shots in Hawaii.

Preparing for the "Brady Kids" tour:
Rehearsals, rehearsals, rehearsals . . .

. . . and more rehearsals!

Joe Seiter helps Mike Lookinland make
a model rocket.

Maureen McCormick and Barry Williams
in an informal moment between
rehearsals.

Mike Lookinland, far from the madding
crowd.

Celebrating Susan Olsen's birthday.

At a wild animal park in Southern
California.

Ann B. Davis gets the monkey business.

The Kids, with their national tour imminent, meet at Maureen McCormick's house.

At the airport in Knoxville, Tennessee.

The big time—Atlantic City's Steel Pier.

The Brady Bunch Kids, circa 1972, in all their finery.

What major rock act hasn't
toilet-papered a hotel room or two?

Barry Williams, on the fringe.

Peter Baldwin directing Mike Lookinland
in "The Brady Girls Get Married."

The grown-up Brady Bunch "kids" with
their spouses/dates at the Schwartzes'
50th anniversary party.

PHOTO AND ILLUSTRATION CREDITS

Front cover (Brady kids), courtesy of Joe Seiter. Front cover (Mike and Carol), courtesy of Personality Photos. Inc., P.O. Box 50, Midwood Station, Brooklyn NY 11230. Front cover (Alice), courtesy of Personality Photos, Inc. p. 9, courtesy of Mrs. Frances Whitfield. p. 13, courtesy of Personality Photos, Inc. p. 15, courtesy of Personality Photos, Inc. p. 17, courtesy of Elizabeth Moran. p. 19, courtesy of Mrs. Frances Whitfield. p. 21, courtesy of Mrs. Frances Whitfield. p. 23, courtesy of Joe Seiter. p. 25, courtesy of Joe Seiter. p. 26, courtesy of Mrs. Frances Whitfield. p. 27, courtesy of Robbie Rist. p. 28, courtesy of Personality Photos, Inc. p. 29, Courtesy of Allan Melvin. p. 30, courtesy of Personality Photos, Inc. p. 32 (top), courtesy of Personality Photos, Inc. p. 32 (bottom), courtesy of Personality Photos, Inc. p. 33, courtesy of Personality Photos, Inc. p. 36 (top), courtesy of Personality Photos, Inc. p. 36 (bottom), courtesy of Personality Photos, Inc. p. 39, courtesy of Mrs. Frances Whitfield. p. 40, courtesy of Personality Photos, Inc. p. 41 (top), courtesy of Personality Photos, Inc. p. 41 (bottom), courtesy of Personality Photos, Inc. p. 43, courtesy of Personality Photos, Inc. p. 44 (top), courtesy of Personality Photos, Inc. p. 44 (bottom), photo by Rose Blume, from the Johnnie J. Young collection.
p. 45, courtesy of Personality Photos, Inc. p. 46, courtesy of Personality Photos, Inc. p. 48, photo by Rose Blume, from the Johnnie J. Young collection. p. 49, photo by Rose Blume, from the Johnnie J. Young collection. p. 51, courtesy of Personality Photos, Inc. p. 52 (top), courtesy of Personality Photos, Inc. p. 52 (bottom), courtesy of Personality Photos, Inc. p. 53 (left and right), courtesy of Personality Photos, Inc. p. 55 (left), courtesy of Personality Photos, Inc. and Jeff Botcher. p. 55 (right), courtesy of Elizabeth Moran. p. 58, courtesy of Personality Photos, Inc. p. 60, courtesy of Karen Lipscomb. p. 61, courtesy of Personality Photos, Inc. p. 63, courtesy of Mrs. Frances Whitfield. p. 66 (top), courtesy of Personality Photos, Inc. p. 66 (bottom), courtesy of Personality Photos, Inc. p. 67 (top), courtesy of Personality Photos, Inc. p. 67 (bottom), courtesy of Mrs. Frances Whitfield. p. 68 (top), courtesy of Mrs. Frances Whitfield. p. 68 (bottom), courtesy of Personality Photos, Inc. p. 69 (top), courtesy of Personality Photos, Inc. p. 69 (bottom), courtesy of Personality Photos, Inc. p. 70 (bottom), courtesy of Personality Photos, Inc. p. 72 (top), courtesy of Personality Photos, Inc. p. 72 (bottom), courtesy of Personality Photos, Inc. p. 74, courtesy of Personality Photos, Inc. p. 75, courtesy of Personality Photos, Inc. p. 76 (top), courtesy of Personality Photos, Inc. p. 76 (middle), courtesy of Personality Photos, Inc. p. 76 (bottom), courtesy of Personality Photos, Inc. p. 81 (top), courtesy of Personality

Photos, Inc. p. 82 (bottom), courtesy of Florence Henderson. p. 84, courtesy of Stephen Cox. p. 86 (top), courtesy of Personality Photos, Inc. p. 86 (bottom), courtesy of Barry Williams. p. 90 (top), courtesy Joe Seiter. p. 90 (bottom), courtesy of Epstein, Wyckoff. p. 94 (left), courtesy of Mrs. Frances Whitfield. p. 94 (center), courtesy of Mrs. Frances Whitfield. p. 94 (right), courtesy of Karen Lipscomb. p. 99 (top), courtesy of Mrs. Frances Whitfield. p. 99 (bottom), courtesy of Century Artists. p. 103 (top), courtesy of Mrs. Frances Whitfield. p. 103 (bottom), courtesy of Epstein, Wyckoff. p. 107 (top), courtesy of Mrs. Frances Whitfield. p. 107 (bottom), courtesy of Susan Olsen. p. 111 (top), courtesy of Robbie Rist. p. 111 (bottom), courtesy of Robbie Rist. p. 114 (top), courtesy of Stephen Cox. p. 114 (bottom), courtesy of Ann B. Davis. p. 118, courtesy of Allan Melvin. p. 120, courtesy of Frank Inn. p. 121 (top), courtesy of Frank Inn. p. 121 (bottom), courtesy of Stephen Cox. p. 124, courtesy of Mrs. Violet McCallister. p. 127 & 128, courtesy Robert C. Greenhood. p. 137 (top), courtesy of Joyce Bulifant. p. 137 (bottom), courtesy of Monty Margetts. p. 138, courtesy of Personality Photos, Inc. p. 139, courtesy of the estate of Jeffrey Hunter. p. 142, courtesy of Mrs. Frances Whitfield. p. 178, courtesy of Hope Juber. p. 179, courtesy of Frank Delfino. p. 187 (top), courtesy of Erin and Don Smith. p. 187 (bottom), courtesy Johnnie J. Young. p. 188 (top), photo by Rose Blume, from the Johnnie J. Young collection. p. 188 (bottom), photo by Michael Lerner at the Toy Patrol. p. 189, photo by Rose Blume, from the Johnnie J. Young collection. p. 191 (all photos), courtesy of Fran & Michael Lerner. p. 194, photo by Rose Blume, from the Johnnie J. Young collection. p. 195 (top), photo by Rose Blume, from the Johnnie J. Young collection. p. 195 (bottom), photo by Rose Blume, from the Johnnie J. Young collection. p. 199 (top), courtesy of Joe Seiter. p. 199 (bottom), courtesy of Joe Seiter. p. 200 (top), courtesy of Karen Lipscomb. p. 200 (bottom), courtesy of Joe Seiter. p. 202, courtesy of Joe Seiter. p. 203, courtesy of Karen Lipscomb. p. 203 (left), courtesy of Joe Seiter. p. 203 (right), courtesy of Mrs. Frances Whitfield. p. 204, photo by Rose Blume, from the Johnnie J. Young collection. p. 206, courtesy of Personality Photos, Inc. p. 208, courtesy of Personality Photos, Inc. p. 210, courtesy of Personality Photos, Inc. p. 212, courtesy of Sherwood Schwartz. p. 213, courtesy of Sherwood Schwartz. p. 215, courtesy of Mrs. Violet McCallister. p. 216, courtesy of Personality Photos, Inc. (photo by Julie Dennis). p. 219 (top), courtesy of P.M.K., Inc. p. 219 (top), courtesy of Elizabeth Moran. p. 220, courtesy of Scott J. Michaels. p. 223, courtesy of Elizabeth Moran. p. 226 (top and bottom), courtesy of Elizabeth Moran. p. 230 (top left), courtesy of Karen Lipscomb. p. 230 (top right), courtesy of Mrs. Frances Whitfield. p. 230 (bottom left), courtesy of Karen Lipscomb. p. 230 (bottom right), courtesy of Mrs. Frances Whitfield. p. 231 (top left), courtesy of Mrs. Frances Whitfield. p.231 (top right, bottom left, and bottom right), courtesy of Karen Lipscomb. p. 232-234 (all photos), courtesy of Joe Seiter. p. 235 (top left, top right), courtesy of Joe Seiter. p. 235 (bottom left), courtesy of Karen Lipscomb. p. 235 (bottom right), courtesy of Sherwood Schwartz. p. 239, courtesy of Rose Blume. p. 240, *The Far Side*, copyright 1988, Universal Press Syndicate, reprinted with permission, all rights reserved.

BIBLIOGRAPHY

Inside Gilligan's Island: From Creation to Syndication by Sherwood Schwartz, McFarland & Company, Inc. Publishers, 1988

Teenage Gang Debs, a fanzine published by the brother/sister team of Erin and Don Smith. It focuses on classic TV shows like "My Three Sons," "Planet Of The Apes," and "The Brady Bunch" (naturally). Past articles have featured an interview with Eve Plumb, an in-depth look at Jan Brady's middle-child psyche, and Cousin Oliver, The Lost Brady. A must read! Send $3.00 and two 29-cent stamps to *Teenage Gang Debs*, Erin and Don Smith, P.O. Box 1754, Bethesda, MD 20827-1754

The Complete Directory to Prime Time Network TV Shows 1946-present by Tom Brooks and Earle Marsh

The TV Encyclopedia by David Inman

Spin Again, a magazine celebrating the world of toys, games, and collectibles. Written by Rick Polizzi. Published by Pilucho Press. For more information write 3400 Greenfield Avenue, #7, Los Angeles, CA 90034.

ABOUT THE AUTHOR

Introduced to TV at an early age, Elizabeth Moran claims that one of her favorite toys was a wind up televsion set that "aired" nursery rhymes. Since her father was an advertising sales executive and her mother a one-time commercial actress, it was only natural that she follow an entertainment profession. Currently she works for KCOP-TV in Los Angeles, where she has been living for the past twelve years. She graduated with a B.A. in Cinema-Television Production at The University of Southern California in 1985.

Suddenly, Dr. Morrissey's own creation, a hideous creature nine feet tall and bearing the heads of the Brady Bunch, turns against him.